Meditation

Grace Cooke
1892–1979

The Golden Key (1929)

Plumed Serpent (1942)

The Shining Presence (1946)

The Open Door (1946)

Meditation (1955)

The New Mediumship (1965)

The Illumined Ones (1966)

The Light in Britain (with Ivan Cooke, 1971)

The Jewel in the Lotus (1973)

Sun-Men of the Americas (1975)

Meditation

Grace Cooke

with White Eagle's guidance

THE WHITE EAGLE PUBLISHING TRUST
NEW LANDS · LISS · HAMPSHIRE · ENGLAND

First published November 1955
Second edition November 1965
Third edition November 1999

© Copyright,
The White Eagle Publishing Trust, 1955, 1965, 1999

British Library Cataloguing-in-Publication Data
A catalogue record for this book is available
from the British Library

ISBN 0-85487-110-1

Chapter decorations by Rosemary Young

Set in 12.5 on 17 and 14 on 17.8 point Monotype Perpetua
Printed and bound in Great Britain at
the University Press, Cambridge

CONTENTS

Introduction to the Third Edition

WHEN this book first came out in 1955 little was commonly known or written about true meditation in the western world. So the book's original purpose was to introduce the reader, and those who followed White Eagle's teaching, to the whole concept of meditation.

For many years White Eagle, with his beautiful teaching, had been leading us along a path of spiritual unfoldment (as it was called then); but it was not a path which included meditation as such—at least not in the way it is introduced and described in this book. Nonetheless it was leading in that direction and away from any connection with the development of psychic gifts. The author, my mother Grace Cooke, had many remarkable experiences of the expansion of consciousness which can come when the mind is still and at peace and the heart open to receive. With her as medium, White Eagle was gradually leading us all towards this deeper and more disciplined aspiration and search.

Then, in a remarkable way, my mother was brought into touch with one from the East who shared with her his knowledge of meditation 'technique' and in sharing his own experience confirmed for her the guidance White Eagle was giving her about the whole art and discipline of meditation. This book came to be written from her own personal experience, in the earnest hope that it would help many whose feet were set upon the spiritual path.

As we have already said it was written as an introduction to the whole subject of meditation, but in fact it is much more than this; it is a book of very deep and age-less wisdom given to us by White Eagle, revealing in its pages also how meditation can open the doors into the spiritual kingdom, the golden world of God. Meditation can lead us to the expansion of consciousness which will reveal worlds of infinite beauty where we can walk with the companions of our spirit, making a real and living contact with our loved ones in that inner world of light.

Today, when meditation is more generally understood and practised than it was forty or fifty years ago, White Eagle's guidance to us is above all to set aside a time each day to meditate and touch the inner stillness of the heart—a time preferably at the start of the day, for the heart contact made then can give us strength and wisdom to cope with the day before us. This individual, rather than group, attunement, is more or less presupposed in the second part of this book.

In the introductory chapters of the book (less so in the second part) the reader is strongly recommended to work initially with a chosen group, and very clear and helpful guidance is given as to the 'ritual', if we may call it that, by which the group should work. The discipline of group work is a safe start and certainly helps the aspirant to touch greater heights and find deeper stillness at whatever stage they are on the path—a discipline which will help them also when later they sit alone.

Perhaps I may conclude this brief introduction by quoting a passage from the book, which in a way says it all: 'Meditation is the true way to unfold the spiritual awareness which is deep in the innermost being. We do not refer to a mental practice but to an awareness which arises from the heart. It is really the awakening and unfolding of the heart centre, by love. Just as a flower unfolds in the rays of the sun, so the heart centre stirs through the daily meditation and practice of divine love.... Then a little light begins to shine upon the path of the seeker for God.'

Our prayer is that the Light may shine upon the path for every reader of this book.

Ylana Hayward

Publisher's Note

THE INTRODUCTORY and connecting passages in this book are all the work of Grace Cooke; however, the major part of the text is taken from White Eagle's own words of loving wisdom given through her mediumship, words of loving wisdom and guidance. For clarity, White Eagle's words are given in the larger type. The meditations on pp. 118, 121 and 155, though included with the White Eagle extracts, are by Grace Cooke herself.

The third edition contains a whole new chapter (chapter five), a teaching given by White Eagle some eleven years after the book was first published. In the interests of clarity, the chapters are now numbered consecutively and the final chapter occupies a part to itself. There are other changes, too, but all are for clarity.

In this new edition, every attempt has been made to render the language gender-neutral. Some problems remain, notably words like 'brotherhood', for which there is no natural replacement. White Eagle is himself ahead of his time in stressing the Father–Motherhood of God. Nonetheless, where it is felt that he is referring intentionally to one or other aspect of the Deity—for example, God the Father as the law-giver or God the Mother as the divine Mother in the natural world—the specific names and pronouns have been left.

Biblical quotations (which are from the 1611 King James version) are set in italics. References to these quotations have been added in this edition, and with one exception all the footnotes are editorial. The exception is the one on page 18, which is Grace Cooke's own.

PART I

CHAPTER 1

What is Meditation?

'Within the Silence one touches the Heart of God.'
White Eagle

TODAY, humanity stands at the crossroads so far as spiritual evolution is concerned. Men and women have travelled some distance on their journey towards their natural goal—that is, to some degree they have possessed themselves of the secrets of nature; but they still have far to go spiritually. What is humanity's real goal? This is a question thinking people have been asking throughout the centuries and are still asking today, especially when sorrow, bereavement or tragedy come into their lives;

for then the question becomes terribly urgent. At such times people want to know: 'What is the purpose of life? What is the good of anything?' and can find no answer.

Throughout the ages philosophers, saints and sages, prophets, saviours and teachers have offered their followers a key which will unlock the door of heaven. The key lies within the heart; and it is love. When the key is used it reveals to men and women that within themselves can be found an 'imprisoned splendour' and a truth which will be the answer to their search. Few will pause in the rush of life to listen to the still small voice which speaks in the innermost heart. This voice which speaks in the heart is sometimes called the voice of conscience, but it is really the prompting of the spirit, the stirring of a *life* or consciousness which White Eagle refers to as the Christ-consciousness. This is found within the innermost or secret centre in everyone, and it is this inner Light or Christ-consciousness that is awakened, strengthened and developed through meditation. By the faithful and constant practice of meditation, together with response to the prompting of the still small voice in daily life and human relationships, the clear vision and clear hearing of spiritual truth begins to develop.

The way is simple but hard, and to progress along it

certain qualities are essential, above all simplicity and humility. Given these qualities, then gradually, as you faithfully persevere in your search and aspiration, that place of stillness deep in the heart, that awareness of the Christ in you, will be touched. You will hear the voice of your Master, the still small voice, the 'voice of the silence' as it is sometimes called.

Within that inner temple of the spirit you only have to ask, to ask of the Christ within, in faith and trust, and you will receive.

By this means those who mourn can receive comfort and solace; and those who are sick in body and mind, or distraught with disappointment and anxiety, will gain succour and strength. The lonely, the sad, the bereaved, the hopeless, can find an answer to their heartache.

You may study the various religions of the world, and read many books, but this intellectual knowledge is not enough. The ultimate attainment must be in the spiritual experience and understanding gained through sure knowledge of the Light of Christ in the heart—in every human heart—its power and its effect on human life and character.

In the East, the aspirant seeks a *rishi* (a holy man) as a *guru* (a teacher or master) and retires to the silence of a holy mountain to find God.* Here, in the Western world, where life is lived very much at the material level, the aspirant must find another way to reach his or her goal and find an answer to the soul's eternal question of the why, the whence and the whither of itself.

Perhaps the secret of meditation can be illustrated by the old Chinese story of Aladdin. Here the treasure hidden in the cave represents the innermost part we all have within ourselves. In this story the greedy intellect is represented by the robber who cannot find an entry into the cave, so he captures by deception the simple and affectionate son of a lone widow (Aladdin here stands for the loving heart) and bids him rob the cave of its priceless jewels. The interpretation of this fable is that, while the intellect cannot snatch the heavenly treasure through any acquisition of knowledge, the treasure can be released by the earnest prayerful search of a simple heart full of love. Afterwards, however, the heart must cherish and safeguard that treasure against robbers.

*White Eagle is my teacher, my *guru*. He introduced himself to me under the sign or symbol of the White Eagle. He has many memories of former incarnations, including an Egyptian, a Mayan, an American Indian, and a Tibetan. His present mission is to awaken the souls of men and women to the light within their souls, and to show them how to develop that inner light for the blessing of themselves and others.

Once, long ago, a Chinese teacher said: 'If a person can be absolutely quiet, then the heavenly heart will manifest itself'.

The ancient Greek philosophers were also aware of this key to the spiritual evolution of humanity. Written above their temples were the words: 'Man, know thyself, and thou shalt know God and the Universe'.

Truth is the same yesterday, today and forever. The ancient Greeks, Egyptians, Hindus, Chinese and early Christians all received from their Masters the philosophy of the voice of the silence which they learned to know through meditation.

Meditation is the true way to unfold the spiritual awareness which is deep in the innermost being of all people. We do not refer to a mental practice but to an awareness which arises from the heart. It is really the awakening and opening of the heart centre through love. Just as a flower unfolds in the rays of the sun, so the heart centre opens through daily meditation and practice of divine love. Then a little light begins to shine upon the path of the seeker for God. This spiritual development taking place shows in the aura, which becomes more illumined as the heart centre unfolds. The aura is a softly coloured radiance which surrounds the physical body. It emanates from the emotions of the soul. Many mediaeval artists depicted it as a halo surrounding the heads of saints and holy people.

As the power to meditate increases, greater light is drawn from the Christ-consciousness, and can be seen clairvoyantly like bright sunlight playing upon the heart centre and radiating from it.

As the warm sun causes the bud of a rose gradually to open, so does the attracted Christ-power, shedding its radiance upon the soul, cause the heart centre to open. This opening of the heart centre in turn increases the Christ love in the soul and character of the aspirant.

Light in the soul is the result of the constant practising of divine love towards every experience which life offers.

For instance, when a person is feeling the emotion of love their face lights up. The constant emotion of divine love or Christ love imparts to the face, and indeed to the whole being, a spiritual radiance. The smile becomes alight with spiritual beauty; the very texture of the skin has the appearance as of a light shining behind it.

Jesus was continually exhorting his disciples to love. The whole Christian teaching is based on the love of human beings for each other and for God. Love more and the inner light shines more brightly. In describing the state of life in which he found himself after death, a friend of mine once said: 'The life over here in this new world is composed of light. Spirit is Light, so we appear to be clothed with light'.

As spiritual development proceeds, the light in the heart centre rises to illumine the head centre. When, through aspiration and the practice of meditation, the light rises from the heart into the head, it brings wisdom and helps in the person's search for spiritual knowledge. If, however, the intellect is developed to the exclusion of love and intuition—which is another word for the guiding light of the heart—then a man or woman becomes hard-crusted, mentally arrogant and almost dead spiritually. He or she is then practically incapable of seeing or understanding spiritual things. But when there is balance between the heart and the head centres a person can move steadily forward towards initiation into the heavenly glories.

It is necessary at this point to explain what is meant by the centres, for the development of psychic and spiritual sensitivity is greatly helped by an understanding of the construction of the etheric body and its correspondence with the physical nervous system.

In White Eagle's method of meditation and spiritual unfoldment seven psychic centres in the etheric body are involved. These are placed at and etherically correspond with the ductless glands in the physical body. The etheric body is an extension of the life-force into a finer ether pervading and surrounding the physical body, and it is more sensitive to the etheric or invisible life beyond the physical. The etheric body carries to the brain, via the nervous system, the impressions or messages it registers from the invisible or psychic world existing behind the dense fog or veil of the physical and material life.

The seven psychic centres are situated (1) on the top of the head (called the crown); (2) between the eyes (called the brow); (3) in or near the hollow of the throat (called the throat centre); (4) on the thymus gland (called the heart centre); (5) at the navel (called the solar plexus centre)—a psychic centre which is a spontaneous receiver of messages from the unseen world often without the person understanding what is happening (children and animals often demonstrate this gift); (6) on the left side of the body slightly above the waist and towards the back (called the spleen centre); (7) at the root, the base of the torso and spine (called the base). At this particular centre the great creative power of *kundalini* lies. It can be the greatest, most holy and mighty power for good. It can also be the root of all evil.

In the practice of meditation we are training ourselves to bring all these psychic centres under the control and direction of the divine will or the Christ-power which lies within the heart centre. Psychic centres can be seen by many who are trained in clairvoyance. The centres are often described as appearing like discs of dull light, situated in the etheric body at the points just mentioned. They are the windows of the soul, the receivers and transmitters of impressions or direct messages from and to a finer life.

When you sit for meditation and for the development of spiritual and psychic or soul-consciousness, the psychic centres are seen to change; they begin to glow with a soft light. This light in time increases in size and brilliance so that the original small disc, with a diameter of about one and a half to two inches, extends to the size of a saucer, and even larger. These centres not only increase in size but start to pulsate with light and to become alive with exquisite colour. In due time, when the soul is highly developed, this disc begins to rotate and will eventually assume the form of a lovely many-petalled flower. Indeed, after perhaps years of meditation and devotion to

God, the psychic centres and the etheric or soul body become a form of heavenly beauty (the body of light) beyond earthly imagination or description. This, White Eagle says, is the destiny of every individual, as exemplified by Jesus, through the Christ within.

The goal of meditation is to bring all the animal, the earthly, instincts under the control and direction of the Christ within the heart and so to achieve at-one-ment or union with God. This means that the human, the microcosm, becomes consciously enfolded in the life of God, the macrocosm, the infinitely great.

So try to feel and express love, compassion, tenderness for all. This is where the visualization of the form of Christ helps in meditation, because in his face and form can be seen and felt supreme love and Light, and visualization of this form helps the aspirant to express similar emotions; that is, to realize that love is pouring from his or her own heart.

Nevertheless, do not concentrate *mentally* upon what is going on in the heart centre, but rather strive through feeling and sharing in the emotion of divine love to expand the heart radiation into the etheric world and thereby to encompass the whole earth with love.

As your development advances, the feeling of love radiating from your heart may bring a sensation of physical expansion, as if the whole body were reaching out in love. This indicates the expansion of the aura due to the radiation of spiritual light through the entire human form. To a very remarkable degree this was demonstrated by Jesus at the time of the Transfiguration, when the disciples watched him talking with Moses and Elias and saw that all three were enveloped in heavenly radiance. This form of spiritual unfoldment, through earnest prayer, aspiration and meditation, is a perfectly natural and beautiful way to develop the psychic or soul senses in full consciousness.

While meditating it is important always to maintain a positive attitude; that is to say, positively to set yourself to attract the good, the true and the beautiful only; and not to lay yourself open to negativity, thereby inviting unevolved astral entities to influence you.

Remember that like attracts like; and what you think and are in yourself will attract to you like forms and influences.

Strive to find the place of utter silence deep, deep within yourself. It lies beneath all thought or thinking. It is not to be arrived at through any process of mental concentration: it is a sweet, simple awareness of the divine

Light, the inner master, the true teacher. The true self, the divine Spirit or Christ within, is ever meek, gentle and yet enduringly strong, just, true and absolutely loving and selfless. Its wealth of love is its real power and strength and its true wisdom.

During your meditation, in the deep silence of the innermost spirit, through your own power of imagery, a temple in the heavens may be seen. Try to remember the details of its structure, both to assimilate and to appreciate the graceful architecture of the tall pillars supporting the domed roof. Note the radiant and transparent texture of the substance of which it is built. You will realize in due course that it is ethereal matter you are seeing, which is like pulsating light. It is indeed light, and it is the spiritual light in you, in your soul, which is used for its construction. Remain alert in your meditation, for you may also hear the sound of heavenly music; yet all the while listen for the true Voice of the Silence.

The walls of the spirit temple are like mirrors, revealing truth to earnest seekers. There may be writing on the walls in words of Light. These are often seen during meditation. Signs and symbols containing a message to the soul of the one who seeks may also be seen. In time you will learn to interpret these symbols, for they are the language of the spirit.

Jesus said: *Ask and it shall be given unto you; seek and ye shall find; knock* (on the door of heavenly mystery) *and it shall be opened unto you* (Mt 7 : 7; Lk 11 : 9-10). This you must do in your meditation, for God can ever be found when sought in truth, simplicity and humility. God is in the heart. The heart is like a well, the waters of which reflect God and truth. Learn to look into the heart to find the key to wisdom and spiritual knowledge, and the answer to every human question.

CHAPTER 2

The Practice of Meditation

WE hope it has been made clear that the motive for pursuing the practice of meditation and spiritual unfoldment needs to be wholly selfless and good. The aspirant yearns to find God and God's attributes of divine truth, love and wisdom. He or she is therefore willing to surrender the desires of the outer or lower self, to discipline that lower self and physical body and to live according to the Christ standard and thus become more receptive to the rays of the Christ Light, more receptive to the Light shining into his or her heart from the Christ Sun. This will be no easy road. On the contrary, it will be strewn with problems, tests and trials.

Nevertheless when you, as aspirant, earnestly follow the way, you will recognize that you are receiving gentle guidance and help; for during the difficulties which you will encounter as you press forward, you are never left without an unseen guide and teacher, who will urge you to be steadfast all the way, faithful right to the goal.

What is this goal? It is the unshakeable, indestructible conviction which comes to the soul during meditation, that you are a part of the whole of life; that you are a drop in the ocean of universal and eternal spiritual life; that you are born of spirit and therefore you are spirit. Your final goal is your conscious union and at-one-ment with God, your Creator.

When this consciousness awakens, the fear of death forever vanishes, for you know that you are part of the eternal life and can never die. Aware of this, you gradually expand from within yourself until you become conscious of nothing else but God. This is what is meant by cosmic consciousness.

Although ultimately your aim would be to put aside a short time each day for your meditation (indeed the time will come when your daily meditation will be an important part of your daily routine), when you are first learning to meditate it can be really helpful to gather together a small group composed of friends who are spiritually of one mind. Jesus told his disciples: *Where two or three are gathered together in my name* (that is, in my spirit) *there am I in the midst of them* (Mt 18 : 20). Let this be your ideal.

When you meet for meditation try to be seated in a semicircle, with a clear space between each sitter. See if a small table can be set or arranged as an altar, or perhaps a mantelpiece can be used. *Ideally*, the room selected would be set apart specially for spiritual work, and used for no other purpose. Think of it as 'the quiet room'. The table or altar becomes a focal point, on which are candles or a small ruby sanctuary lamp, flowers and perhaps a picture of a Master or Saint hanging above the altar. The reason for an altar is that it symbolizes the communion table, a place where there is a concentration of spiritual power and beauty, waiting to be received and absorbed by the aspiring soul. You could alternatively sit in a circle with a small table altar at the centre of the circle.

When all are seated, the correct posture should be observed; each one should sit comfortably—relaxed but with the spine straight. Let each one imagine that they have a piece of elastic fixed to the crown of their head*

*Technically, although the sense of connection between the crown centre and the heavens is helpful, the part of the head that the elastic should be

with the other end attached to the sky; thus giving the illusion of being gently (with no strain or tension) held upright by a power from above.

The right ankle should be loosely crossed over the left and the hands lightly folded in the lap, right under left, with palms turned upwards, so that the left hand is lying cupped in the right hand.

When all are sitting comfortably upright but relaxed and at ease, some recorded music, preferably wordless, quiet, harmonious and uplifting, will help to raise the consciousness of the sitters above earthly things. During the music, gentle rhythmic breathing, slightly deeper and slower than normal, will be a further aid to detachment from the earthly self; but this controlled breathing must not be allowed to become so slow or deep as to create strain or discomfort, or to excite coughing or a choking sensation; nor must the breath be suspended. The breathing must remain calm and easy with a gentle, soft inhalation and exhalation. As you breathe in, imagine that you are breathing in, absorbing into your being, the spiritual sunlight of Christ. As you breathe out, feel an

---

seen attached to is nearer the back of the head. If you imagine the spine continuing straight up from where it finishes, this will be the right place for it to be attached.

outpouring of Light from your brow and heart centres, praying that the Light may bless and heal humanity.

Now all is harmonious and the group is attuned to a spiritual vibration and life. The leader then quietly reads a selected passage from a suitable book. The reading should be short and should serve to raise the group still higher above normal consciousness.

Bear in mind that in your meditation you are seeking the place of absolute stillness and silence *within*; so the sitters should train themselves to sit motionless and to restrain any fidgets and coughs which will not only disturb themselves but also the whole group.

Some people may prefer to sit alone for meditation. There is nothing against this; indeed, as already said, your daily meditation alone, in the quietness of your own prepared place, will in time become an essential part of your day. Nevertheless, it can be helpful, if possible, at least in the early stages to join with others, because a concentration of spiritual power gathers in a group, and each sitter can both receive from and give help to the others. When sitting alone, try, as far as possible, to follow the same procedure as for a group; and also make sure that you will not be disturbed by any sudden knock on the door, the entrance of another person, or the ringing of the telephone.

It should be remembered that the first step towards meditation is sincere worship of and devotion to the Great White Light, because this particular method of meditation is designed to encourage the growth and expansion of the Christ Light in the human heart. Devotion to and love for the one who is the Master of Love will assist in the opening of the heart centre and the awakening of the Christ in you. During your meditation persevere with this practice of dwelling on the enfolding love of the spirit of Christ. Search for that spark of light within yourself, for this will surely shine amidst the darkness. If necessary, use your power of imagery to create this light in your consciousness. See it shine out like a jewel, glistening and pulsating with lovely colour and radiance.

If and when you can do this, remember it is only the beginning of the real awakening and development of your spiritual vision or clairvoyance. Accept this light as your starting point; then, as development proceeds, its gleam will grow ever brighter, and presently expand to a sun-like disc looking very bright and beautiful. Remember that all this will take place *within yourself*, and is to be seen subjectively, not objectively—with your inner vision but not with your physical eyes. The next phase will be to imagine yourself going right into and through this disc of light; and then (still using your gift of imagery or spiritual imagination) to visualize yourself as entering into another world, a new world created out of finer ether (which is itself a kind of rarefied light).

Remember, the beginning of all life was Light. *In the beginning ... God said: Let there be Light: and there was Light!* (Gen. 1 : 1, 3). Out of *Light* everything that has form was made. In the same way, out of the little light that you first conceive during your early meditations, everything that *is* in the etheric or spirit world (which will presently reveal itself to you) will be created. In meditation you are therefore first made aware of the reality of Light. This Light is essentially the Light of God, from God, from which all subsequent vision, revelation and experience is born. If you are sufficiently earnest and constant in your spiritual work and aspiration, without question you will finally succeed in passing through the veil which separates this dark material world from the more beautiful state of life which is the spirit world; you will become aware of the world of spirit which is all about you and within you.

If the steps outlined are faithfully and patiently followed, the inner self and the soul of the seeker will in time be able to disentangle itself from its dark prison of materiality and become conscious of itself as part of the essence of God.

The way of meditation set out here has been given to us by White Eagle. It is purposely made plain and straight-forward so that anyone, however inadequate he or she may feel, can begin work on the development of his or her spiritual vision, the vision veiled within the heart where dwells the Christ seed-atom. This way of development is also a safe way, for it guides the soul by the Light of the Christ love within, gently and without strain.

This short book is the result of practical experience, extending over a long period and with many pupils. It presents only the beginning of a path that can lead you up to the heights in heaven; although the way is never easy.

Other methods of meditation are used in the East. The one outlined in this book is designed for people of the West; and is based on devotion to 'the good, the true and the beautiful'; and to finding and serving the best that is in us and in our neighbour.

It has been emphasized that the path is not easy. The search for the Light can also stimulate the darker side, and awaken inharmonies in the lower or earthly mind, and conflict ensues. For this reason warning is repeated that the motive in seeking spiritual development and unfoldment must remain pure and selfless; and self-discipline regarding daily living and thinking must become a habit.

If your mind should wander during meditation, constantly and resolutely bring this wandering mind back to thoughts of the compassionate figure of Christ, making this the focal point throughout the period of your meditation. It can help very much to have a little still flame burning—a candle or a night-light on which to focus initially. The process of preparing for meditation and the continual practice of this ritual before entering into spiritual communion will greatly assist in the continuity and success of your communion.

Having established this inner and powerful soul-contact with the finer worlds and those who live there; having dwelt with them for a brief time in communion and worship and learning, the time will come for a gentle but definite withdrawal from this inner world.

White Eagle teaches us to be as clear and precise in our method of withdrawal as we were in our approach to the heavenly state of consciousness. During meditation powerful forces may be released within the soul, which can form strong attachments with out-of-the-body life and people; therefore it is important that an equally powerful and correct ritual should be used to ensure the complete return to earthly consciousness; and to close and seal the psychic centres against any possible intrusion by undesirable influences or entities from the astral plane. The procedure is like closing and locking the doors of your home. You do not leave windows and doors unbarred when you are going to sleep at night—at least not if you live in a town. Your commonsense tells you it is necessary to protect yourself against intrusion. It is exactly the same with the astral world. We must be very wise and prudent; for while we can live with our head in the heavens, our feet must still be firmly placed on earth, and we must look to see where we are going.

Therefore, to close our meditation, we must gently but deliberately turn our faces away from the heaven world in which we have been dwelling, to return to consciousness of the physical world. The leader of the group, after about twenty minutes (for a beginners' group), or a longer time for a group well established in the art of deep meditation, should tell the group that it is now time to return to physical consciousness, and then gently but firmly lead them back. It can be quite helpful, after a pause, to say together the Lord's Prayer. Then the leader should direct the sitters in the group to seal every centre or chakra by mentally making the sign of the cross of Light within the circle of Light and seeing it laid upon each chakra—the crown of the head ... the throat (this lies just in the hollow of the throat) ... the heart (the centre of the breast) ... the solar plexus (just above the navel) ... the spleen centre (under the floating ribs at the back, on the left hand side) ... and the base of the spine, the sacrum.

The meditation is concluded by 'drawing the seven-fold breath'. That is to say, the sitters breathe deeply and consciously a series of seven breaths: on the inhalation the Light is envisaged as being drawn up the left side of the body from the foot to the head, and then on the exhalation the Light passes over the top of the head and down the right side to complete the circle—a perfect oval of Light which conforms to the shape of the aura and seals it.

Having done this, the sitters then draw in a deep breath and as they do so imagine a spiral of Light beginning at the feet, and then rising clockwise, encircling the body seven times up to the head. By this time the lungs will be full: upon their release, the line is seen to pass right down through the body, through the centre of the spiral, and into the ground, 'earthing' the sitter.

At this point it is appropriate for the leader of the group to say a short prayer of thanksgiving for the blessing received during the meditation.

This ritual of sealing can be adjusted according to the length and profundity of the meditation. For instance, after the personal 'quiet time' every morning, just to do the sevenfold breath, encircling the body in Light, would be quite adequate, especially if you were able finally to envisage the protective circle of Light as a 'cross within the circle' with the six-pointed star at its heart—as the Star is at your heart. The same may apply after a simple public group meditation.

White Eagle has said that between Jesus Christ and St John is a sacred and holy bond; and that the church of the new age is the church of St John. He says that in the new Aquarian Age (which is now coming into being) a mystical and truer interpretation of the four gospels will be read, and understood by every man and woman once they have found the key to set free their pure inner psychic or soul powers. The particular work of the Masters on the sixth and seventh rays, the Master Jesus and the Master 'R', who are now both close to humanity, is to train and teach us how to unfold and use the spiritual gifts that are needed during this new Aquarian Age. The Book of Revelation, assumed to be by St John, tells of the visions which came to him while he was raised in consciousness to a state of illumination during his meditation. He says as much in these words, *I, John, who also am your brother, and companion in tribulation, and in the kingdom and patience of Jesus Christ, was in the isle that is called Patmos, for the Word of God, and for the testimony of Jesus Christ*. Again, *I was in the Spirit on the Lord's Day* (in a state of exaltation) *and heard behind me a great voice as of a trumpet* (Rev. 1 : 9, 10). And again, *After this I looked, and behold, a door was opened in heaven: and the first voice which I heard was as it were of a trumpet talking with me* (Rev. 4 : 1).

These, you will see, are the visions of a great seer while his soul was exalted.

Again, 'Know thyself,' said the Greek philosophers, 'and thou shalt know God and the Universe'. The Church of St John (the symbol of which is the White Eagle) is bringing to humanity a religion of true brotherhood, spiritual vision and understanding of the esoteric, or inner, aspect of Jesus Christ's life and teaching.

Meditation is a sound and safe method by which you can unlock your own inner power: but only if you will be wise, and keep true to your higher self while pursuing your path.

CHAPTER 3

The Divine Fire:
Meditation in Daily Life

Now, some words from White Eagle, who says:

Let us think of the human soul as being, in the beginning, like an uncut jewel. Through various experiences undergone by the soul on earth, that jewel is being slowly but surely cut and polished. Each facet of that jewel represents an age of the soul, a period during which the soul has been developing and perfecting one special aspect of itself. If you can grasp this idea you will readily see that men and women can appear to be more spiritual at one time (or during one age) than in another. One aspect of the jewel is being cut and polished. Then, with the passing of time, another aspect of the soul (or the jewel) comes to be cut and polished; so that while, at one time, it is the perfecting or growth of the emotional body, at another time it may be the growth of the mental body, and at yet another the development of the celestial body. In this way the human soul passes through various stages of unfoldment, and may appear at one time to be very spiritual and at another very material. Yet in due course the soul learns to balance the two aspects of God, which are called good and evil; and in its higher initiations the soul realizes that what may be considered evil in one age may not be so in another age.

Eventually, understanding of this big problem of good and evil comes. When rightly viewed so-called evil is seen to be caused by the *destructive* aspect of the Creator; its purpose being to break down old conditions before a fresh growth can take place. This is what we mean when we say the soul learns to balance these two opposites of good and evil.

Souls on earth are like children at school. One of the lessons they learn is that if they put their hands in the fire they will be burnt: but, because fire burns it is not of itself evil. The soul has to keep all these forces of life in their right place and use them for good.

We remind you that during your meditation you are going into the temple of your inner self. It may feel to you as though you are going out of your body. You may feel a sensation of movement, which will appear sometimes to be like the movement of a spiral. While this is happening you can at will, in a flash, call yourself back to your body. At the same time, you will also feel that if you allow yourself to continue you could go a great distance away from your body. This will be difficult for you to understand, but what is really happening is that you are going *inward*—into the temple of your own self where the power of the divine fire is hidden. The temple is itself built of the divine fire, usually called the fire of *kundalini*. The meaning of the word *kundalini* is a 'bowl of fire'. *Kundalini* is sometimes represented as the serpent which rises from the bowl—the fiery serpent. Now, the serpent in its higher aspect is wisdom; but it has a lower aspect as the tempter. Thus in the story of the Garden of Eden the serpent rose up and whispered to Eve, the woman.

The woman, in symbolism, means the soul, and the higher serpent power is in every soul as the divine fire. Mostly it is asleep, dormant; it only awakes and arises in the soul as its evolution quickens. It then whispers to the soul, telling it of the power which God has given it to choose its actions, to select the experiences it will undergo.

God is omniscient; God does not make mistakes; the law of God is just, perfect and true. Men and women have been given the power to choose their actions; they have yet to learn to choose rightly. When they do something wrong they discover eventually that the result is painful to *themselves*. Only by exercising the power of freewill can humanity learn this. They will never learn from teaching or from instruction from others while their souls are young. They will only learn from their own experiences. God is all-love. By giving human kind this power of choice, God was giving to all humanity the greatest gift that could be given.

The following brief passages are included because their object is to awaken us to reality concerning ourselves. Meditation, we shall find, is so real a thing that we must become real ourselves to practise it. White Eagle says:

In the degree that you aspire to God, so you will manifest God's beauty and love in your outer life. What a wonderful mission is yours! Your purpose in this present incarnation is to bring through God's glorious Light and beauty in order to beautify the world around you, and to enrich your own life and the lives of all who come near you. The purpose of your incarnation is for the Spirit to use your physical life for the greater glory of God.

You see, we are all partners with God; we are also God's servants and God's children. Keep on thinking this thought and it should help you to live more joyously and more thankfully. Those who live, as it were, shut up in a prison, do not know of the wonderful spiritual organization which overrules the outer life. All things work together for good for those who love God; it cannot be otherwise; for God's cosmic law ensures that *what is good in a soul draws good to itself.*

Whenever we talk to you about the nature of time we find that you are all at sea in your thinking. You begin to think about ages and ages of time, about millions and millions of years; but this really means nothing. Can we help you by saying that human life itself is really only the period of your consciousness in time? That in reality there is no time; that your sense of time is all a question of your consciousness? Life comes to you and you live; presently it leaves you and you pass out of physical existence. Your body apparently decays, but in reality it is only changing its form and, in various forms, will exist for ever.

Now, if you can once get into your minds that

there is no such thing as death, and that life when the soul is fully conscious, although it may change from one level to another, is eternal, and there is no death, then you are finding truth. This can happen when you are in meditation; when in a flash of illumination you touch the level of cosmic consciousness; for then you will surely know that life is eternal, that life always has been and always will be; and that *you are that life*. Therefore you cannot die; you will never die. Only when you touch that level of cosmic consciousness will you realize the eternal truth that life changes form but never dies.

Those who would learn to meditate are called to prepare for a spiritual work. This work is to glorify God by thought, by word and by action—by thought so that henceforth you may think kindly, purely and lovingly; by word that you may speak gently, kindly and truly; by action that you may always perform your tasks as perfectly as you can. There must be no slipshod methods. The mind, the speech and the action are three avenues through which to let the perfectness of God express itself.

Some may think that to see beautiful things is all that is required; or that it is only necessary for them to think of God occasionally and then close down the shutters. But God means us to think, to speak and to act continually with the quality of Light, the quality of the Christ-spirit. Whenever this is said, the response often comes that 'we are only human'. No, not so; we are all essentially divine; we are indeed sons and daughters of God the Great White Light. We are, ourselves, Light; and our mission in the world is to make the Light shine in the darkness.

Beauty is always a manifestation of God's harmonies. When we walk in the fields and in the lanes we can see this manifestation in every flower, in every blade of grass and in each bush and tree. Even then only a part of the beauty of God can be seen, yet many people are blind even to this. So it is well to cultivate the power of observation. Only when you are quiet in spirit do you have time to observe the shining loveliness of the dew on grass and flower, the exquisite detail of an insect's wings, the delicate colourings of wildflowers and the sheen of sunlight through the trees. As you unfold you will be able to observe the nature spirits at work in grass and flower, bush and tree; and to walk in fellowship with water, wind and sunlight. You will then enter what the children call the fairy world. Remember in your meditation to look through outer form to see the spirit form within or behind the physical. For instance, when you are meditating you may see stones or rocks; try to penetrate these rocks with your inner vision. Then you will find yourself in an enchanted world, in an Aladdin's cave; and you will see the stones shine like jewels, rare and beautiful in colour and texture. You do not yet realize what a world of beauty lies hidden within the world of physical matter. The true clairvoyant has the joy of seeing this beauty revealed.

There is one truth of which we can assure you: once you have opened your vision to the spiritual life, once you have opened your heart to admit the companionship and guidance of the angels, *you will never be left without their help*. Go forth into the world with this assurance in your breast, and an inward and constant knowing that in the degree you serve God, all is well. So also in your service to humanity will you receive the blessing of the spirit of joy and peace and love. This golden Light is even now shining on you all. Be filled....

Let us make clear that we do not agree with the practice of mortifying the flesh. We believe instead in its purity, and in manifesting through flesh the supreme and perfect Life. We believe in the heart being filled with sweet, compassionate, and gentle love, so that the mind does not criticise others or the heart become embittered either by life or with the companions whom one meets on one's journey.

We say, therefore, keep your vision continually

on the Light; let this become for you the Holy Grail; let nothing obscure your vision; keep on your journey with your heart devoted to your purpose. In this way you can save yourself from much unnecessary suffering and pain, and save your companions likewise from stumbling or falling by the wayside. It is rather an overwhelming thought, my children, to realize how much we are all responsible for the faltering and failing of our companions on the journey.

The Master has said that one of the essentials for a disciple is to reach a state of dispassion, a tranquil state of being. Nothing delays the progress of a soul on the path so much as a lack of dispassion. It is perhaps easy to enter into this state while you are living in prepared and harmonious conditions. But it is not so easy when you return to a world of turmoil because, although you may try to retain inward peace, you are still subject to the violent vibrations of humanity in the outer world. Nevertheless, dispassion is something which every disciple must attain, for without it he or she cannot maintain close communion with the Master. On this is built all true and devotional work. So, while you seek to meditate let all outer things fall from you: surrender your mind, your soul and your body to the joys of the spiritual life, and in time you will be able to remain dispassionate even in the turmoil of the outer world.

Light is eternal. Darkness and evil are transient. Light is eternal because it forever recreates. Darkness and evil are transient because by their very nature they destroy. The mythical phoenix is a symbol of this eternal Light which eventually has to be absorbed by the supreme Light. Only one principle is eternal and this is the principle of Light, of Good, of God. Put in another way, although there are the two aspects of positive and negative, the negative is ever subject to the positive and is eventually absorbed into it.

Follow the example of the carpenter's son, the son of Mary, the divine, the perfect, Mother. The carpenter, being a good craftsperson, must work with perfect tools. The good craftsperson measures up their work, and everything about their work is just, perfect and true. The symbolic figure of Jesus as the carpenter's son reveals to humanity the significance of this perfect craftsman. It means that there must be no slipshod methods in working, even with physical material; still less can there be slipshod methods in working with the substance of which the higher planes are constructed. Only when the craftsperson—and *you* are that person—has, through repeated incarnations, to a degree perfected his or her craft can he or she truly meditate. With each succeeding incarnation, you should become better fitted to continue your life on a higher plane. Until you are perfect in your craft you cannot perfectly operate on a higher plane, because you would not be able to handle its substance.

CHAPTER 4

Creative Imagination
The Testing · True Communion

DURING the course of many years White Eagle has led his pupils along the path of spiritual unfoldment. It is hoped that this book will be a further guide to those who are ready and willing to find for themselves the treasures of the inner temple.

The following are extracts from White Eagle's teaching about meditation and related subjects. They are a way to prepare your mind and to give you a background for your meditation.

The average person is very set in their ideas: we are not condemning or blaming anyone, but we recognize that men and women generally have one-track minds which continually go over much the same ground. Encircling this one-track mind is so much that is wonderful—beautiful scenery, a glorious existence about which they know nothing. That may be the reason why your own life often appears difficult and lonely; why you feel as though you are always toiling, as of course you are! It is because you so seldom look up that your feet grow heavy and the track along which you are driving yourself seems rough and stony. How many sad people have said to us, 'Oh, how I wish I could believe in God!' My dear child, the proof of God is within you! What more do you want? Do you not know that you are eternal and that your Creator is all love; that there is nothing to fear in death; that you can never be separated from loved ones? Do you want to be sure that in your meditations you are not deluding yourself; that you are not just imagining something which looks attractive but is really a delusion?

About this you say, 'Yes, I seem to be carried away when I meditate; and afterwards I seem to come back to earth and find reality'. What you find on your return is not reality; it is illusion. Your whole physical world is a world of illusion, and not at all what you think it is. For instance, can you believe that your world is in truth built out of Light? Do you know that your own body, could you but see it with clear vision, is also composed of Light? No—surely not; only when you rise in consciousness during your meditations and aspirations do you move into something which is lovely and eternal. Oh, the wonder of the Breath of the Infinite, the perfume of that Breath, the joy of that real Life! Can this be something which really disappears in the cold light of day? We answer that all that is holy, all that is pure, sweet and lovely is of God, is therefore real. That is your *real* state of life.

On hearing about these things people will say: 'Then why are we down here, imprisoned in this heavy body of ours? Why is our sad world in the state it is if our lives could become so radiant? If this world has ever been like the Garden of Eden what has happened to it since? What have we done to bring about this state of existence?'

Yes, what have you done? Or rather—*What are you doing now?*—that is more to the point: because if you lived every moment in the consciousness of your Creator, in the consciousness of the Son of God, of the Christ, you would no longer be battened down in darkness, nor would you suffer. The love of God is your real creator and it will (if you will allow) create beauty and harmony in your body and in your surroundings. It will give you a rich inner spiritual life which cannot be hurt or sullied by the illusory outer existence. You will answer, 'That is all very well; but it seems that however admirably we order them our thoughts cannot alter material conditions; neither can we make other people do what we should like them to do'. No, you should not try to do the latter. Let other people do whatever they want to; they must learn through their experience, as you have to learn through yours.

Jesus once said: *I am the Light of the World* (Jn 8 : 12). How do you interpret this saying? Do you think it means something supernatural? Jesus cannot mean that he is really a light—as on a dark night? But he does mean exactly that. *I AM the resurrection, and the life* (Jn 11 : 25), he said. The 'I AM' which is also within each human being throws out a light from the heart, and that light penetrates all mists and darkness.

Proud of their reasoning minds, human beings do not intend to be misled. This manner of thinking indicates that the lower mind is dominating the higher. Even those who are learning to meditate do not wish to be deluded by what they call 'imagination', by that creative power which is (did they but know it) their greatest gift; because, if they were bereft of their power to create mind-images there would be very little left for them to create. Have you ever thought that your whole life is directed, your every action is urged by reason of these mind-images? You have first to imagine your clothing, your house, your food, your agriculture, your everything, before you can bring any one of these into being. Your every activity has first to *become* in your imagination. Where there is no vision (or no power of imagination) the people perish, and indeed they must perish. What is vital is that the imagination, the aspiration must grow Godward. God is beauty, therefore God creates all beauty; God has created you, therefore through you, God's creation, beauty must become manifest.

The vital subject of the imaginative powers must be deeply studied and so come to be far better understood, because imagination is truly the doorway to all your creative powers. It is primarily a spiritual thing and so opens up a higher world. We have often said that all your imagining must be pure, beautiful and Godlike; because this is how you will create yourself anew, in body, mind and soul.

Some people think that to meditate means just to sit, just to think beautiful thoughts. This in itself will not get you very far. Correct meditation brings knowledge, because it releases the soul from the bondage of the physical and mental bodies; it enables the soul to rise through the various planes right up to the high peak at which illumination comes. This sort of illumination brings with it universal knowledge. In this manner the soul practised in meditation learns to approach the Temples of Wisdom; and there, in the silence, it receives from the teachers the knowledge and understanding it seeks.

In meditation the secret is to get beneath all thought. Do not try to *think* your way through to anything or anywhere. Try instead to get beneath the surface of thought, beneath emotion, to the place of silence. When in that place of silence it is essential for you to visualize or imagine form. We will presently explain the reason for this; but first we advise you to centre all your thoughts, prayers and aspirations upon God; because at the beginning of your meditation you need to rise to higher planes of consciousness and so to become united with your higher self and the celestial body. In the celestial body is stored the memory of all the past good which has been built into the temple of your soul. This is why it is essential to ascend to a high peak of spiritual aspiration when you commence meditating. In other words, you rise through all the planes of consciousness—through the lower astral, the astral, the lower mental, the mental, right to the celestial or, as some people call it, the 'Christ' state of consciousness. It is at this point that, eventually, divine illumination comes, and you are no longer limited by a personality; you merge into the Infinite Life. This is what is called cosmic consciousness, but it does not mean that you will lose your individuality. What really happens is that the little individual self expands to permeate the universe. At that moment there is no limitation of any kind and the soul receives knowledge of every plane of its being.

This is why we are taught to seek first the kingdom of God and told that all things shall then be added. This is why we are taught to follow the Light of human and divine love, for that is the one true Light which raises the little self up to become united with the greater self. At this moment there is a union between the pineal and pituitary glands of the head.* Then comes a wonderful expansion of consciousness; but the soul with its life and duties on earth cannot remain in such a state of exaltation and illumination. After a period of ecstasy it

*There is further useful teaching by White Eagle on this subject in WALKING WITH THE ANGELS, pp 44ff.

has to come down again, but bringing with it something of the radiance which has illuminated its being. Several stories in the Bible tell of the attainment of cosmic consciousness; and the most outstanding is the Transfiguration—when Jesus was seen by his disciples to be illumined by heavenly Light. There is also the instance of the apostle Paul, who was struck by a flash, as if of lightning. This again was an instance of divine illumination and an awakening of the cosmic consciousness.

You will feel that any such state of consciousness is far removed from you, but you are wrong. The reason people seldom reach it is that they are pulled down by desire for material things, by desire to have their own way, by the mind of earth which brings forward all kinds of clever arguments to explain why they should remain earthly. To reach the heights the soul has to pursue its path of aspiration ceaselessly. It need not take very long for the soul to receive divine illumination if it be steadfast and purposeful. There are many instances of saints who have attained this desired end; but it does mean giving up all selfish desire, and this is the hardest thing of all because the pull of earth is so strong. Nevertheless, even this pull has its purpose, for it makes the soul which strives against it strong and beautiful.

When meditating try to let all thoughts of earthly things fall from you, and concentrate your whole soul on the glory of God and on the Son, the Christ. Always yield to the upward pull of the divine Light and truth. Dwell awhile in that state of ecstasy, of worship; and then after the period of communion (which may last for only a minute or two at first) you can commence visualization.*

When you first see anything, your lower mind will try to argue, and tell you that you are making it up. It will say, 'This is all imagination and cannot really exist; you are deceiving yourself!' This is always the method of the lower mind, but the truth is that you cannot imagine anything that really does not exist. You may think you can; but if you visualize, say, a

*Today, meditation is often taught in the White Eagle Lodge using visualization at an early stage, to quieten the mind and open the heart to beauty. What White Eagle means here by visualization is something slightly different, as the next paragraphs indicate.

picture of some sort, the very fact that you can visualize it means that you are producing it out of the substance of your own soul. For if the picture is vividly in your soul it exists, it is true. You cannot produce anything in your imagination which has no existence, because if it had no existence you could not imagine it. We remind you again that all things which exist in physical matter are a product of the imagination. Physical objects originate in the imagination, and then they are made in the physical world. So also is nature the expression (or the manifestation of the imagination) of beings who work for God. Thus, the great Angels of Form labour continually to produce on earth the array of beauty which you call nature. People, unfortunately, can and do misuse their power of imagination and sometimes produce cruel and ugly things; but all form is the result originally of imagination, or of 'spiritual' creation.

Some day you will live without a physical body and then you will create and control your own conditions or environment. You do not realize that what is in your soul is already taking form in the spirit world. When you have shed your physical body all you will have left is what has taken form in the higher ethers *from your soul*. The world that some people go to is an unpleasant place because they themselves have created that unpleasant condition in their soul. Others go to beautiful conditions which they are creating through their soul-substance by the power of their imagination. So, all that is thought about and thereby created in the mind takes form in this and in the higher world, and lives and remains there.

The reason you are all so afraid of imagination is that you do not understand what it truly is. Therefore, when in meditation you see incidents from some of your previous incarnations (as some of you will) do not torture yourself by thinking, 'is all this only something I am imagining? Am I making it up?' That again is the lower mind, the mind of earth that would destroy your realization of the beautiful flowers of the spirit. In the temple of the celestial body is a storehouse of memory of all your past lives. What was good in those past lives is stored and that which was dark and unwanted in time falls away and disintegrates.

So, whenever you see pictures, whenever you imagine them, you are seeing clearly, you are using the faculty of spiritual clairvoyance. Do you not see that the substance of your vision, of your imagery, is already in your soul? If it were not there you could not create your picture.

So also, when you meditate, you cannot err if you work from the truth that is within, from the love that is within, right out to the outermost of your circle. In your spiritual consciousness you have an unlimited range of places to visit, of temples which your soul has helped to construct through aeons of time. If you do not use your imagination, you may become dimly aware of a Light and a peace, but will remain static. What you must do, then, is to bring your will into action. Your will must cause you to go forward into your world of imagination; and in time the truth will become clear to you that what you are visiting is a real world, a world of spirit. Seek for those things which are beautiful and Godlike and you have no need to fear. Your life will become enlarged, your soul will become beautiful to others and you will be a true servant to humanity.

We say again, put your lower mind on one side when you meditate. It is your enemy; it is trying to shut you out from the kingdom of heaven. Put your hand into the hand of the Master and let Him lead you through the gates of initiation into the universal temple of beauty. When the leader of your meditation group suggests to you that you might imagine a temple of the Brotherhood, and gives you one or two hints—such as 'Look at the pillars, look at the arches; examine their substance, the material of which this temple is constructed'—go with your leader and imagine these things. Then follow your own path. This is the point where you must bring your power of imagery into operation, and imagine what lies beyond the temple walls, or visualize beautiful souls filing in and taking their place before the altar. Imagine from your heart what that altar is like; and because your soul has already visited that place it will produce for you a picture of that altar. It will be true because, as we have said, if it were not in your heart you could not imagine it. Whatever you imagine has its root and life in your soul and is built from the soul-substance.

When you meditate you are rising unconsciously through the spiritual planes of your own universe. According to your karma, you may even be allowed to reach the planes of records,* but do not try to force an entry. Only at the right time will you be allowed to see your past lives or some incidents in them at least. Alternatively, some of you may dream about a past life and will retain the memory of your experience in the Hall of Records. These things must come unbidden at the right time according to the karma you have made. If the soul contacts the Hall of Records while still living on earth it means an initiation has been passed; or in other words, that an expansion of consciousness has taken

*i.e. of stored karmic memory.

place. Afterwards there sometimes comes a reaction and a closing down. This will only be a temporary condition, so do not be cast down or disappointed. Accept what happens in humility and in faith, for the Lords of Karma act under divine intelligence and command.

Let us now meditate together. We are sitting in a semicircle in a temple; its canopy is the blue sky. The pillars of the temple are the trunks of trees and its carpet is the little flowers. We can hear music: the music of the grand organ of all nature. Its harmonies are composed of the songs of birds, of the wind in the trees, of the rushing of great waters and the gentle song of burbling streams. We see all around us spirits clothed in shining garments and wearing jewels, particularly on the heart centre. The heart centre itself is always likened to a blazing jewel, for when it is fully developed it sends out rays of exquisite colour.

The stately grandeur of the trees makes a pathway

for the vast throng of souls. They move up this pathway towards the rising Sun, singing from their hearts the praises of their King. In the blazing disc of the Sun we see the Presence, the manifestation in human form of the beloved of the Father–Mother, the spiritual form of the Cosmic Christ. Around the Christ form are pure and lovely souls whom He has gathered within the shelter of His wings. Now we see that the golden disc has also wings, as of fire, and has become the winged disc of the ancient days of Hyperborea, of Atlantis and of Egypt. Reaching forth from Christ are the everlasting arms and you can find not only strength within them, but also rest and perpetual renewal. Then every obstacle in your path can be surmounted; indeed, every obstacle is absorbed, is melted away by the fire of the love which radiates from the winged disc which is the symbol in the heavens of the Cosmic Christ.... How little now are the troubles of your outer life! They seem now as specks of dust. They cannot remain; they all pass. What will abide with you is the memory of the eternal glory, the Life, the Sun, this truth, this beauty, this everlasting happiness.

In this way we are blessed, for God has entered in and taken part in our meditation together.

Let us ask, what is faith? Faith is an inner knowing of God, or surety of spirit. Prayer, true prayer, is faith; that is to say, if you pray rightly you are praying in faith; you have faith in God or else you would not pray. Faith comes to the inner self as the result of a flash of insight, or illumination. Once you have had this flash—we do not mean astral clairvoyance but true spiritual enlightenment—once you have had this experience, afterwards you will be tested to see how strong your faith is. Here may we say that since your faith will be tested, so also it is right, just and logical that you yourself should test the truth of any inspired teaching.

Any wisdom which comes through from the spiritual side of life should withstand any testing. The words of the Master should stand up to any trial your reason as well as your intuition can devise.

Truth is spiritually scientific fact. The ancient wisdom that flows from the lips of sage and seer is heavenly truth. Thus, while you are being tested regarding the quality of your faith, so also, by reason of your experience of life, you become able to test the truth of the scriptures, and indeed of all spiritual teaching. Your faith will then be complete.

The soul of every man and woman passing through the world has to tread a path similar to the one the Master Jesus trod. He was the vehicle through which the Lord, the Cosmic Christ, manifested. We look therefore to the life of the Master Jesus for understanding, for knowledge of our own particular path. We notice that Jesus, after receiving a divine illumination in which the voice of his Father was heard calling him 'My Son', was caught up and saw the glory of heaven. There are people who have had a somewhat similar experience, having seen a vision of spiritual truth and of the life beyond the physical. Having seen a vision of spiritual truth and of the life beyond the physical, they have felt elated, full of joy. They have said, 'This is it! This is truth! I shall never again be unhappy or fearful!'

Then comes the test. After this wonderful spiritual illumination, they may find themselves back in even a worse mental state than before. They are wandering in their wilderness, as did the Lord Jesus. They cry for spiritual food and cannot find it. They pray, and there seems no answer. They wander for forty days. The number forty is used several times in the Bible, as when the Israelites wandered for forty years, and Jesus spent forty days in the wilderness. This period is likened to the period when the babe rests in the womb of the mother before its birth. What is meant is a period of confinement in darkness and powerlessness; a condition in which the soul must wait 'for the acceptable time of the Lord'. It is impossible for the soul to rush forward. It has to learn to be patient until conditions are exactly ready. Have not you come up against this in your own life? Fettered, confined and cramped, have you not longed to break out, and been unable to do so? And then all your chains seemed to fall away without any particular effort on your part, except a stepping forward when the opportunity was given. Having made your move, you thought, 'Why could not I have done this before? Conditions are unchanged, and yet then I felt that I could not stir. Now everything seems simple and easy.'

What we are trying to point out is that you cannot force any conditions. You must realize that whatever comes, comes with good reason and purpose. It comes to enrich your soul with spiritual wealth, to bring a deeper and truer quality of spiritual consciousness. When Jesus was in the wilderness Satan came to him and tempted him in much the same way as you are tempted today. The devil is a symbol of the earthly, the reasoning mind. This mind has its purpose, but you must recognize it for what it really is. The reasoning mind tempts you to discard all spiritual teaching and striving, saying, 'Why should you struggle to attain realization of truth, true knowledge and development? You might just as well live on the outer plane like most other people, and save yourself effort.' In this manner the tempter tries your true, your higher self. It will also argue: 'If this spiritual teaching is any good it will give you power over material things. Test it now!' This test is a very subtle one. Jesus had it, in that he was tempted to turn the stones into bread to satisfy his mortal self, his physical hunger. The stone, here, is the symbol of the Christ-power. The term 'stone' is used several times in the Bible. Jesus is called the cornerstone, or the keystone of the arch through which every initiate must pass into the heavenly world; or into the eternal truth of life. So he was tempted to turn the stone into bread for his own advantage.

This is what a lot of people often do, unknowingly. They do not mean to, but when they approach understanding of the wonderful teaching of the Christ, they realize that here is a definite and dynamic power, and try to use it for their own ends. Initiates, on the other hand, learn that it is wrong to divert spiritual power to satisfy their own worldly needs, or even to convince the unbeliever; neither must they make themselves seem greater in the eyes of the ignorant. This sacred power (symbolized by the stone) cannot be turned to material advantage. But Jesus said: *Get thee behind me, Satan* (Lk 4 : 8). That was spoken to the lower mind tempting him to misuse his powers. He said also: *Seek ye first the kingdom of God ... and all these things shall be added unto you* (Mt 6 : 33). This teaches us to serve God before Mammon.

This way of the spirit is *your* way, my brother, my sister, because you have in the past seen into the heavenly world and the way of life there. Through this vision you receive faith. Yet although faith may dwell within your innermost being, your reasoning mind still tempts your inner self to betray its master, the Christ.

You may live a long time before you become tempted to betray the Lord Christ within—for a whole incarnation—but tempted you will be. Yet there will come a stage, we promise you, when the soul can be tempted no longer, because it has come into close communion with its God. Thereafter the soul is filled with hope, joy and inner certainty that God is love, that all things work together for good, and that God will never forsake it. Some who read

79

our words already know by many demonstrations that God never, never, *never* fails. God never fails to feed you both spiritually and materially. God is all good, all wise and all loving. We do not mind what you have to tell us about the gravity of your present conditions. We still say that hope is your anchor. If you have confidence in God you have hope. No one can take that hope away because your soul has learned that the world cannot really touch you.

The real *you* is quite apart from the body. Realize that you are spirit and are at-one with your God. Therefore *nothing* on earth can permanently hurt you. If you are confident in God's love you can live out your days in peace. You can go happily about your business when it is also your Father–Mother's business. You can give out Light and service and love all other beings, and remain untouched or unmoved by anything that the material life can threaten or do. If you suffer from any bodily disease you can be sure that your disease has come as the result of a broken law, perhaps in some past life. This breaking of the law may be due to ignorance on your part—that is the ignorance of your ordinary mind; but your deeper self is aware that suffering has one object only—which is to bring to you experiences which will educate, develop, and evolve your soul. So, when you have passed the initiation of faith you hold fast to a steadfast hope which no one can take away. Nevertheless, you are told by the Sage that at the last something even greater than faith or hope stands out. This is *love*.

We see many varying demonstrations—or shall we say manifestations—of love on earth. Love is Light. Love is the Divine Fire, and love is Life. Love is God. God is love. Christ came to manifest through the body of the Master Jesus, saying, 'I AM the Light of the World'. 'I AM the love.' Now love is the Light, the warmth and the sun of all life. From within and behind the physical sun above we can receive into the whole of our being, the Light of the spiritual Sun, the life of God, and so renew our spiritual life. Indeed the soul cannot grow very far without love.

Love is the great solvent of all difficulties, all problems, all misunderstandings. Try it. Apply love. Apply love by your inner attitude towards any human problem. Put aside the reasoning mind. Let love, divine love, operate in you. Give out from your inner self God's love, and you will be surprised to find how simply every problem will be solved, and how easily every knot will be loosened.

The Sages of the Brotherhood of the Star, or the Elder Brethren, say there are those on earth who know; there are those on earth who do not know. Therefore let your prayer be, 'From the unreal, lead me to the real'. It is of vital importance that you pray and seek to be led away from the unreality which is of the world and all its claims on the senses to the reality of the other world. Cry, 'Lead me to the real!' for the real is spiritual and glorious!

If you really want to know the complete satisfaction to be found in perfect communion with the world of spirit, and with your own beloved in that world, you must leave aside all the semi-material methods of communication because they are illusory. The one way which is true and unfailing is the way of meditation. Some of you will now say to us, 'Meditation does not seem to help me. Indeed, I find that I cannot meditate.' Very well, then; you must work on your own plane as long as it satisfies you; but we are speaking of things which are ever true and beautiful. To these you must some day attune yourself. You must leave the outer world with all its attractions, and turn inwards into your heart chakra (or centre), which is like a temple of Light. You must learn by the patient method of attuning yourself to the Eternal Light, which is the Source of your own spirit. Turn inwards; contemplate and meditate upon the God within. You will in time become aware of this centre of Light in your own being; and that same centre of Light is not confined to you alone, for as it unfolds it reaches out and it touches the universal. Then you become *en rapport* with radiant beings whom you love to contact.

Remember that your own loved ones after passing through the astral planes go onward, and then they too become conscious of the celestial world. In that celestial world you can meet them face to face. Never make the mistake of thinking that because you dwell in a body, you are limited to the material world only, and have to attend only to material things. You are divine as well as human. You have a celestial body as well as a physical. Your celestial body has been given you to use even while you are operating through a physical body. It is a great error to think you cannot reach the glories of the heaven world. In the course of evolution, you have to learn to go as a traveller, as a visitor, to your true home in the celestial world; and there see for yourself the glories which God has prepared for every soul who loves the spirit of truth and who loves God.

Meditate often on things which are Godlike. It will not make you sanctimonious and pious but more radiant, and more truly a brother and sister to the man and woman by your side. It will bring to you health, harmony, happiness. You can choose no greater, wiser path to follow than this for your evolution, and to develop all the God-qualities with which you are endowed. Sit daily for a short time in earnestness, in truth, with no thought of self or material needs but only of the Great Spirit. Spare God five minutes out of your day; you can afterwards meet Him–Her as often as you like. Remember you can meditate all the time; that in the heart chakra you can always be active and aware. Meditation means the attunement of your spirit to the Great Spirit. When you have accustomed yourself you will become aware of that point of Light which we have described, which is really your heart chakra. You will find that Light will open out for you a world of beauty, wherein you will meet beings of perfect spiritual life. They are always ready to smile, to be happy with you. These are the sort of companions you will meet in that place of true communion.

The place of communion, as we have said again and again, is the temple within your own being, of which the Master Jesus spoke; indeed which all Masters through all ages have taught their pupils to seek, a communion in which you eat the bread and drink the wine of life. The Holy Grail, dear ones, is here within the heart; it is also the universal cup. May you patiently pursue your path; you will surely get there and you will know the joy of life, for all the mists will clear and happiness will be your crown.

Choose always the way of the spirit. This does not mean becoming all airy-fairy, of dreaming dreams and seeing visions: it means putting into practice the law of brotherhood; putting into practice the spiritual law of life.

So, in thought, word and deed strive to live the life of the spirit. Beneath all sound, beneath all thought, is the eternal sea of life, the eternal Now. Seek to become acquainted with that Now. Live in the consciousness of the eternal and you will lose your fears. What does it matter if foolish men and women follow sidetracks which lead them nowhere but back into the jungle? *Your* task is to be true to that unnameable power and life which is within, which is all around you, as it is also in the heavens. If, when you leave your body, you have worked to disperse all the mists of materialism which gather round you, you will then be living in a state of Light. O, my children, we would draw back the veil between the worlds! Human form may change (as it also does in our world) but the quality of the Light *never* changes, even for the denizens of the spiritual world, but grows ever more radiant and beautiful, ever more satisfying. Children, take no thought for unreal things which wear you out, which break you down, which bring continual pain, suffering, and mental anguish to you. Seek first the kingdom of God, the glory of the spirit.

'All this is very well', you will say; 'but what happens when the test so stretches us on the rack that we think we are going to break, so that sometimes our faith fails?' Even then you must hold fast to faith, for at the end of your endurance the Light will come and your need will be supplied. God never fails His–Her children. Divine love supplies all your needs; it is the whole of your life. So *take no thought for the morrow.* Why, even the lilies in the field are clothed in the glory of God! Solomon, the earthly king, *in all his glory was not arrayed like one of these.* Again, not even a sparrow falls to the ground but your Father–Mother God knows it: because the sparrow is a part of God, a part of the whole. Therefore *the very hairs of your head are all numbered* (Mt 6 : 34, 28-29; 10 : 29-30). Only the mind of the earth can separate you from God, by denying Him. God is ever-present, always watching, always bringing good, bringing Light and life forth out of nothingness.

We pray for the blessings of the Light to descend into your hearts, and that you may resolve to follow the Star of Christ, and so come to recognize that those things which are invisible, those things which are spiritual, are verily the real things which shall never be taken away.

From the unreality of earth lead us to the real.

From their darkness lead men and women to Light. Amen. Amen. Amen.

CHAPTER 5

The Secret of the
Golden Flower

There now follows a complete teaching by White Eagle.

WE like to use the Greek word Christos for the Great White Light, the Christ Light. But we notice that many of you are not yet clear what we mean by the Christos. It does not matter what religion you follow, what scriptures you have studied, behind the scriptures of all the ages lies this fundamental truth—the light which came into the darkness of matter; and the whole purpose of man's many incarnations is to develop *within physical matter* this beautiful light which we call the Christos: in your language, the Christ-spirit. It is within all religions, no matter what name you give it, the same light. The White Brotherhood consists of these souls who are able to use intelligently the power which that Great White Light brings to them.

We would now call your attention to the duality that runs all through life—the positive and negative, light and darkness, good and so-called evil. We say 'so-called evil' because when it is seen rightly it is recognised as a force that has its part to play in the general balance of life. This is one of the secrets of the ancient wisdom—the balancing of opposites. In human beings the pull is between spirit and matter. In early stages the soul on earth is unable to balance that pair of opposites and there is a strong pull to physical matter. A large number of people are immersed entirely in material things. They have no use at all for the invisible or intangible; they say it does not exist. On the other hand, some souls seem to be imprisoned in matter because they are bringing back certain conditions they have created for themselves in the past; thus they *appear* to be imprisoned for a time, but they are learning through being bound in a state of materialism. You are on earth to learn to balance these two opposites, the spiritual and the material, and in this great lesson you will see the meaning of the perfectly balanced triangles of the six-pointed Star.

As you come to recognise this, you may begin to think about the inner power of the light, and how to use this power. Now you may know a lot of things with your brain, but the one secret you cannot know with your brain only is *how* to use inner or occult power effectively. This secret culture, or the development of what they called the 'Golden Flower' within themselves, was known to our brethren in the Far East.

Now let us touch for a moment the two aspects of life in religion. In all religions there is an outer and an inner truth. The masses know only the outer aspect, and interpret the words of the scriptures according to their own ideas. Yet there are others who, being a little more evolved, begin to see that there is an inner and an esoteric meaning which deals with the soul, and with the development of these occult powers within man. For instance, in the Revelation of St John these secrets are to be found, but of course the active mind only reads words and only interprets in a material way the meaning of these sacred revelations which were given to the beloved saint. This Ancient Wisdom is to be found in all the scriptures but it is veiled and not yet understood. You have to undergo certain experiences on the inner planes during meditation before you can catch a glimpse of the true wisdom in the ancient scriptures.

Today we are endeavouring to help you to find this truth within yourself, not through the development of the mind and the activity of the brain, but through your soul, through meditation. We are not now going into a deep dissertation about meditation, but most of you will know that the truth we are referring to is the positive development of the creative power, which can be directed and drawn up through the etheric and physical body right into the dome or the highest chakra, called by our brethren in the East the thousand-petalled lotus, where it brings illumination. Yet even in this development we get the opposites—on the one hand the pure and the good wanting only to use this power to glorify God and to bless and help all creatures; and on the other, the baser beings who have not yet found the light, who would use this power for what is called black magic to dominate others. On the one hand you have the white magic, on the other hand the black.

Again the blending of the two aspects is required. We do not mean that you should ever use this power for black purposes. We mean that the soul has to learn how to control and use this power by drawing it up from the lower chakras of the body right up into the dome or the highest point, the apex.

In your meditation we direct you first of all to go right up to the apex of the golden triangle and there meditate on the Great White Light or the Golden One, the Christos. As you go directly and earnestly to that point and focus your worship, your adoration, your consciousness in that universal and infinite Light, you must at the same time bring all your devotion, all your power to that one supreme point. This creates in you the perfectly straight line of light from the base of your spine to the crown of the head, like the mason's plumb line. Not only is your body straight, and the power rising straight up through your body, but all your concentration is on God, on what is good, what is lovely, what is beautiful, what is true, just and wise—the whole being is brought into poise, into straightness.

This same teaching is to be found in masonic law, the 'building on the square,' which means to build on a foundation of truth and rightness, with all the virtues of the true Brother expressed and manifested in your life. That is building on the square. The ancient Egyptians had this truth, when they built their pyramids on a square foundation with the triangle pointing up to the heaven, symbolising the divine spirit, the Eternal Flame of life. In human terms, it simply means that you are honest, true, sincere and loyal.

Remember again the two aspects of life—the outer, which is your everyday life, which must be clean and wholesome and straight and good and kind, and also the inner. Now you are learning by slow degrees how to bring into operation the power of the Golden Flower. Sometimes you say you cannot see anything in meditation—but that is never so. It is impossible for your mind to be a blank. Some say you must make your mind a blank, but this is an utter impossibility. You can keep your mind at peace, which is a different thing. You must keep it still and at peace, but you must centre it on something. You must have your mind either on God or on Mammon, on material things. It cannot be a vacuum. Therefore in meditation the very first thing to do is to think of God. If you would then visualise the Star, we advise you to see it on the point of the triangle because that immediately lifts you up into the Star, which you must imagine or visualise.

When you have really gained mastery over the physical body, the nervous system and the thinking—so that in all ways you can create the condition that the divine will within you wishes to create— then you are able, when you sit in meditation, to build round you 'the temple of the Golden Flower', exquisitely formed of spiritual or celestial substance. In meditation you are fully open like a beautiful flower, like the thousand-petalled lotus of the head chakra, or the many-petalled lotus of the heart chakra. You as a spirit are actually *in* that flower, and that flower builds up all around you in the form of a most beautiful temple, a spiritual temple. You are then in the temple of your own soul and spiritual world.

Now let us return to the projection of the Star, which you visualise at the apex of the golden triangle. You not only visualise that Star but you *are* that Star. You are the soul poised on the apex. You are in a higher state of consciousness, and all around you has formed by your own spiritual development, by your devotion, faithfulness and loyalty, the temple of the Star. You are in that temple of the Star, and even as you wish to send out help and light and healing, this beautiful power is going out from that Star of your creation.

Every one of you is your own creator, your own saviour. We mean by this that you have been given freewill. You can create outside exactly what you are in yourself. And when you come to the spirit world, all the beauty and love and selflessness and devotion which you have poured out on others in your life, you find reproduced around you in your spirit home. Many souls when awakening on the astral plane, say, 'All I can see is God. God in the flowers, God in the trees, God in form, God in the landscape, God in everything!' Yes, 'I am in God and God is in me. We are inseparable.' And yet each one retains his or her individuality. All the beauty of God flows through the individual, and the more Godlike the individual is, the more beautiful his or her surroundings and appearance. One who is God-like is in every way a channel of God.

When you wish to send out the light of the Star, do not merely force it out from your brow chakra. Open yourself in humility, sweetness and love to the Christos, to the one who is called Christ. Man or woman made perfect is indeed the perfect Son–Daughter of God. That is the meaning of the word 'Christos': the Christed One. There are a number of Christed Ones on earth now. There have been a number of Christed Ones throughout the ages because there must always be Christed Ones on earth; otherwise the earth would not be saved. It is this Christed spirit which is the salvation of human kind. When you want to send out the light of the Star, try first to get to that feeling of love in your heart. Jesus said so simply, 'Love one another.' *Love the Lord thy God with all thy heart, and with all thy soul, and with all thy mind, and ... thy neighbour as thyself* (Jn 15 : 12; Mt 22 : 37, 39). Upon this law hangs the whole of spiritual evolution.

So we love God. We raise our thoughts to the apex of the Golden Triangle and visualise there the glorious Star. We hold that Star, that point of light; and in that point of light, right in the centre of that perfect geometrical six-pointed Star, we may hold the image of anyone we desire to help. Or we may just hold the Star and see the rays raying forth. If you do this properly and in sincerity, in truth and in belief that what we tell you is true, you will succeed not only in helping your patients, helping the world by sending out light into the darkness of matter, but you will at the same time be developing within yourself that lovely Golden Flower and be living in the Star Temple.

This is the secret: To live, to know and *to be*, to be in the consciousness of the Infinite Love and Light, and to live for spirit and not for matter. Matter is secondary; spirit is the first and foremost in man, and to live rightly you must live to develop the consciousness of the Great White Light or the Christ within yourself. Not in the brow, my friends, but in the heart, and in the thousand-petalled lotus at the apex of your triangle.

Work always with this higher triangle, and the Star. The triangle is in the Star—your triangle on its base, and the balancing triangle of your higher self penetrating, coming down to unite and form the Star.... You are in it, and you have to become aware that you are in it, and you have to develop the consciousness of the power of this Star to perform miracles. But remember it is not *your* will when a miracle is performed. It is God's power; it is God's will. Only God works miracles. God is the light in humanity, and God alone gives or withdraws according to His–Her wisdom. We hope you understand that and will not force what you think ought to be done. Surrender, my children, surrender to God's will in all things.

PART II

THE LAKE OF PEACE

Arise out of yourself,
Let go the garment of the body:
Seek the place of healing silence and tranquillity,
Seek the lake of peace within,
Calm and tideless.
Let the boat of the mind glide slowly
    from its moorings
(Leave the turbulent, restless river)
Past the soft green fingers of the rushes,
Into the lake's cool silver,
Quiet rippling at the prow.
Here the unruffled heart must wait.
Wait not impatiently for the long-sought action,
The eager self outstretched to grasp
And to hold tightly.
Wait gently—as the water waits
For the cool touch of light upon its
    moving stillness,
For the pulse of the evening air—
Steadily beating.

There is calm here and awareness of nature,
So be tranquil and aware of God.
Though the hand of time is still closed to
    your desires,
Let go desire for it is the measure of your
    uncertainty,
Your lack of faith.
By the clear light of aspiration
You shall see:
You shall see there is peace in acceptance
That His will may be done.
Rest in the timeless centre of your being,
The dwelling place of wisdom.
When you are ready
The appointed hour shall come.

                                    T.D.

CHAPTER 6

In Thy Presence is Fullness of Joy

THIS book is designed to help you to reach a point in your search for the spiritual path where you can truly feel, and become deeply conscious of, the eternal presence of God in your soul, and recognize divine wisdom in the order and outcome of your personal and material life. Therefore it is suggested that you read it slowly, contemplating each chapter as it comes, rather than reading quickly through as you would a novel.

Except where otherwise stated, the readings quoted here are extracts from talks by White Eagle. One of them (or a similar reading) well-absorbed into the higher consciousness, may precede any attempt to enter into that deeper meditation or contemplation of the spirit world, which is part of the search for spiritual truth.

While you must make proper preparations before entering into deep meditation, conscious union with God does not really depend on the outer conditions you set; and this is one of the great truths to be learnt in spiritual training. Most of us feel a human urge to *go somewhere* to escape from those inharmonies which appear to block our approach to God: but the truth lies in ourselves and not afar off. We have to practise the art not only of self-sacrifice but of self-surrender to God. Immediately we can do this, surrendering to this inner truth, or life, and thereby 'feeling' the love of God or the nature of Christ well up within and around us, we know a deep peace. We know it the instant we surrender our own desires and earnestly pray, *Thy will be done!* (Mt 26 : 42). Then we begin to understand the love and the wisdom of God, which command all good to come to us.

I knew a woman who after a long, hardworking life found this secret of the white magic; and her response to the contrary events in her daily life was, 'Well, if God wants it this way, so be it'. She accepted the way God caused things to happen in her life. 'This is God's way', she would say, 'so I joyfully accept it'.

Nevertheless, choose the time and the conditions most suitable for your meditation. Arrange to be undisturbed if you are meditating on your own. This may be difficult for you; but it is essential to feel free from interruption, because sudden disturbance could give a psychic shock, which, to say the least, is unpleasant. Perhaps late at night or very early in the morning will be your best time. If you are not meditating in a group but have a room set apart in your home as a 'quiet room' or sanctuary, this is ideal (see the earlier suggestions in chapter two). Also, sit with your spine comfortably erect and hands lightly interlocked, or cupped with the left hand lightly resting with palm upturned on the right hand, also with palm upturned. This forms the shape of a cup, or, as it is sometimes called, the lotus. Breathe calmly and rhythmically, slowly visualizing within yourself the dawning spiritual Light, and in it, the form of the Lord Christ. Absorbing this Light and this gentle, loving nature—that is, 'feeling' that your true nature is the Christ nature, worshipping and adoring the perfection of life that comes from this being—you can then feel welling up within you the intense joy of the spirit.

This gift for feeling joy is part of our Christ-nature. In our meditation, we see ourselves and our world in a Light which floods our being with joy.

We find within us a Presence which opens the way into worlds invisible and glorious.

We are bathed in joy, we touch the loftiest height of human and spiritual joy. Our being sings with joy, dances with joy.

We find that life itself is joy, and we are reborn into a tangible world of joy. As the Psalmist sings, *In Thy presence is fulness of joy* (Ps 16 : 11).

The regular practice of meditation is a certain way of unfolding your inner spiritual powers, and training you in the projection of streams of clear and pure thought to your Master. It is an aspect of the work of meditation to establish this conscious link with the Great White Brotherhood, who are God's messengers to this earth plane from higher spheres of life. Through constant devotion to your regular meditation, the link between you and your Master and the guide of your spirit is established. Be not weary in your effort, for I can assure you that, if you are motivated by a pure and selfless desire to be a servant of the Master in helping humanity to rise out of its spiritual slumber and materialism, you will without doubt evoke a quick and powerful response from your spiritual guide, who is the messenger of the Master to you. Every soul who can make the effort to arise and 're-turn to the Father' is like the prodigal son.

Meditation and sincere, pure spiritual aspiration invoke the help of those Great Ones who are always watching for an opportunity to help those who are younger on the path of progressive enlightenment.

Each individual soul has within itself the power to send forth spiritual Light which can heal the sick in mind or body, and establish on earth peace and 'God-will' amongst people and nations. Thought-power is the greatest power in life. Send it forth mentally by visualizing a six-pointed Star of Light many times during the day and always at some point in your meditations, remembering that the Christ-spirit within your heart is the Light. By such thoughts you yourself become, on the etheric plane, a great Star of blazing Light. The series of short readings in the next section, which are followed by a theme for medi-tation, are intended to help you in your life's work. They have been given by White Eagle and selected with this object. They can be used for daily or weekly meditation by groups or individuals as circumstances permit, but the necessity for regular practice is emphasized.

The White Magic

When you read the words of Jesus, *I AM the way, the truth and the life, I AM the resurrection and the life* (Jn 14 : 6; 11 : 25), remember that Jesus was conveying to his listeners that the life within him was the power. If only you would live by that inner power! It is the Light which lights every soul on the path to the kingdom of heaven.

Jesus was endeavouring to convey that God has planted this Light within you. Live by that Light and it will bring to you love and life and power. You let trivial things absorb you instead of going right to the Father– Mother in heaven and saying. 'Mother, Thou knowest my need; Father, work through me, let Thy power flow through me!'

You would find that the power within you would work like magic, and instead of being strained and weary you would be buoyant and light and joyous, and you would be filled with this power of life.

I AM the true vine.... The Father is in me and I am in Him (Jn 15 : 1; 10 : 38).

These are not just idle phrases. Absorb and realize

them, and they will release you from the earthiness of the flesh and all the material conditions in which you find yourselves.

Why be anxious, my child? Your Father–Mother knows your need. Live in accordance with the law of life and be at peace.

God the Father has His messengers to carry out His law. Remember this and do not think that you are the law. Do not think you have the power to put things in order as you wish them to be, but remember that the Light, the God within you, is all-powerful.

Let the presence of God in you, working every day in office and shop and home, carry you through the journey in matter towards the state of life which is heaven.

You should not feel weary in body or mind if you endeavour to realize this glorious Light and Presence, which is within you always.

Meditation

In the deep, deep silence we find God....

Not in the mind, not in great activity, but when

all is still and a great peace is upon us, then we find ourselves in that place of peace before the shrine, the blazing throne of God.... God who has the qualities of both Father and Mother, the will and strength of the Father and the wisdom and love of the Mother....

In the presence of God there is born from the human heart the Child, the Son, the Light, the Christ.

Let us ever remember the secret way to find God and the Light....

In all Things be Temperate

In all things be temperate. Be wise; keep your poise.
The spiritual life must be balanced by the practical,
for the aspirant, through mastery over practical affairs,
must manifest the wisdom, the harmony and the tranquillity of God's spirit. You are not here to dream your
life away, but to beautify life and to enjoy all the gifts
which God gives you. The well-balanced man or
woman, seeking to glorify God, will use his or her life
to be happy and to make others happy. Follow the Son,
the Light in your heart, the voice of Christ, which is
gentle, not arrogant. Be calm and trusting. Do not get
agitated about tomorrow, for tomorrow will take care
of itself. One step at a time; but when taking that step
be full of joy, for your Father–Mother is by your side
and all is well.

May the peace of the Infinite Heart bless and sustain every action and thought of your life.

Meditation

We would raise your consciousness to the Golden
Lodge which is above all other Lodges in its beauty

and wisdom. There see the pillars of golden light reaching far up into the heights. See through the Golden Royal Arch the communion table spread with the pure white cloth.

Now, into our vision comes the form of the Christos, the Lord Christ.... He bids us partake of the Holy Communion which He is offering....

From His brow He brings forth the bread, the symbol of the substance or essence of all form.

From His heart He brings forth the goblet of wine, symbol of His life-force, of the magical life of Christ.

He calls upon the Father–Mother God to bless both the substance and the wine of life; and He says: 'Take, eat the bread—absorb it into your consciousness, into your soul. It is My cosmic body shared with you, for you are a part of My body.'

He raises the goblet filled with the wine of life, which is the spirit of Christ. 'Drink; let it flow through your body and soul; it is of one spirit, for you and I are one in God.'

Hear the company of shining souls chanting: 'Holy, holy, holy, Lord God Almighty, heaven and earth are full of Thy praise.

'Glory, glory to Thee, Almighty Presence, for all beings live in Thee, and can live only by Thy love.

'Amen. Amen. Amen.'

Constancy

The Great Spirit enfolds you and upholds you in the power of love. This power works in the heart of every man and woman when all has been resigned to its wisdom.

If you would be responsive in the fullest degree to the rays of light from the Elder Brethren, you must learn to be very calm and gentle in thought, word and action. As the still water reflects the sky, so the calm soul reflects the image of Christ. Be still within, be tranquil. Hold yourself in calm certainty of the reflection in your life of Christ's image.

The Presence of the Lord Christ is with you.... We speak individually as well as collectively.

All that you *will* to do, first dedicate to the honour of God, and then the power to accomplish it will be given to you. In the degree you become filled with adoration and reverence towards your Creator, your heart will glow with the Light of the Sun-life within you. Understand that all power is given to the soul who loves God, the power of love to understand. It can illumine a room when the soul possessing such a love enters that room. It can illumine a whole country when a great soul is guiding that country. The power of love uplifts, and points the way to God. The power of love brings deep happiness, unfading beauty into a life. The power of love overcomes all obstacles and indeed all darkness, since no darkness remains when love grows strong in the human heart.

So, however hard your task seems, whatever burden you carry, whatever trial you feel lies before you, with all simplicity and humility pray to God; and then the Master will come and the power will arise in you, and you will accomplish all things in the name of Christ, the Lord of this earth planet.

Love is the king of kings! Love is the lord of life! Therefore, children, love one another. Love life, love every task which comes to hand. Love is the fulfilling of the law, and until the law is lovingly put into operation you cannot know the joy which God holds in His–Her hand to bestow upon all humanity. The law is Cause and Effect. Sow love, goodwill, peace, and you will reap likewise. Love is God's law fulfilled.

O God, may love abide with us all and guide and inspire us every moment of our lives; then indeed will love triumph over death and the curtain of the temple will be rent, and all people will see revealed in the Holy of Holies the mystery of God and love. Love is the fulfilling of the law, the completion of life.

Meditation

Let us humbly pray to be raised in consciousness to the Great White Temple, to the assembly of universal Brotherhood in the heavens.

May we touch the deep, deep Silence; May we receive the blessing of the Almighty Presence, the God Presence....

Let us be *still* ... and know God; God in the beauty of all nature; God in the gentle love and healing of Christ—the Son, the Light in humanity; *Let the Light shine forth*!

Overcoming the World

Jesus once said: *I have overcome the world* (Jn 16 : 33). The mistake many people make is to fear that conquest of their lower self is something which cannot happen for a long time. You think, 'Perhaps when I get to the other side, or when I have had a few more incarnations, I will do better'. That is your mistake. If you fall down many times on the path, you must pick yourself up, you must call upon inner strength, inner light and power. If you are sick, never believe that because doctors say so, there is no cure. Believe us when we tell you that with God all things are possible. There is no real choice—you must keep on keeping on in faith. But do you know what real faith means, what faith really is? Faith is an inner knowing, an inner certainty. Once you have reached that inner certainty that the Christ-spirit can overcome all weakness, sickness and sin, hold fast to it; then you are winning your battle. Also, do not believe your healing will be too difficult. Divine love is waiting for everyone who will accept it and share in it. Christ in you can arise and overcome all weakness. Do not even talk about your sickness to others unless what you say is going to help someone. Banish sickness from your thoughts. Reach beyond the mortal body into the higher life of the spirit. Feel that you yourself are rising without your physical body, rising as on wings into the heavenly states, into the heart of the Sun. There is a tremendous outpouring of life-force from within the Sun; golden rays are pouring down upon you even now. Wait … accept … be filled.

Jesus said: *Thy sins are forgiven thee. Go and sin no more* (Lk 5 : 20; Jn 8 : 11). The Christ in you forgives, forgives all your mistakes. He is the saviour of all your life, the healer of all infirmity. Attune your earthly self to the higher self and to the heart of the Solar Logos continually; every day and many times a day open your inner consciousness and see the great circle of golden radiance emanating from the Sun. In its centre is the Heart, the Christ-spirit, Source of all Light and truth and health. When you feel the Christ glory pouring into your soul, you are readjusting, recreating, bringing about harmony in your being. Then you can only feel love. At that moment you are perfect because in Christ you cannot remain imperfect.

Surrender yourself to this glorious Son of God, the lifegiver, the health-giver, the peace-bringer. There is nothing in you which cannot be healed. Love is here and waits for you. Realize that this pure divine love enfolds you all. None is excluded. Cease to be anxious about material things. You cannot serve two masters. This is so very necessary for you to understand, believe and live, if you would progress on the spiritual path.

Do not permit yourself to be dragged down by doubts or fears. The power is strong, it is mighty, it can accomplish all things; for it is God and God is supreme.

Meditation

Let us take for our meditation a blue lake or pool of healing.

The pool is set in the heart of a perfect garden where flowering shrubs and beds of massed flowers in soft shades of blue and mauve can be seen.

At either end of the pool are white steps leading down to the water, and at the steps stand angels of healing waiting to receive you and assist you into the blue healing waters.

Suddenly you find you are alone, for the angels have withdrawn; but a certain faith or trust or belief has taken hold of you, and you glide through the healing bath, and seem to be lifted by unseen hands on to the soft green lawn.

All pain has left you. You feel no discomfort. The water has not appeared to make you wet. You feel warm, dry and so light and free from all disease. You are in your spirit body, and it is perfect....

Hold firmly to this thought, and the spiritual healing will be transmitted to your physical body.

Thank God and the ministering angels for this experience. This is one way of receiving the healing rays.

CHAPTER 7

The Golden One

FROM time to time White Eagle has made reference to 'the Golden One'; and it is in answer to repeated requests as to the appearance and nature of the Golden One that this is written, and to exlain an experience in meditation.

When attempting to write of this invisible Essence of the heart of life one is baffled through lack of words with which to express the almost inexpressible. Nevertheless, it is necessary for us to try to comprehend in human terms a universal Being of infinite love who, for the purpose of manifesting to humanity, chooses a form which the children of earth can recognize and understand.

To think of the Golden One instantly raises the mind to a higher level. The conscious thought suggests to the mind's eye sunshine, a place of sunshine, which gradually takes form, a golden form. In this manner one's mind, soul and spirit slowly absorb rays of incredible loveliness. Nothing seems to matter, nor even to exist outside this aura of golden light, which has miraculously risen from a secret fount within the soul. The same golden radiance surrounds us in space, and we are compelled to the realization that we live, move and have our being in the Golden One. We visualize this immanence in the form of a blazing Sun, and we feel the outermost points of the rays of this Sun pierce our heart, inspiring adoration, devotion and love to life, to all creation.

But, you will ask, is this all that is meant by the name? Is it just an invisible and, to most of us, an indiscernible essence? Or has it, as the name implies, a personality?

With spiritual vision, we see the perfect human form in the very heart of the blazing spiritual Sun.

We are told in the scriptures that the second person of the Trinity was the 'Logos': the 'Son', and the 'Word' of God.*

*Strictly speaking, the scriptures do not define the Trinity. It was one particular school of thought in the centuries following that identifies

The events which appear in all the stories and myths of the ancient sun deities, we find have been retold in stories and myths in the Christian teachings of Jesus. The Christ of the Mysteries is the Solar Logos, the spiritual Sun behind the physical sun. The Golden One is the second person of the Trinity, the Word. The Golden One is also the second person of the divine spirit in man—woman, hence the universal Christ—a being who symbolizes divine being, and who also represents a fundamental truth in nature.

This was ever the teaching of the mystery schools of all the ages past: this was the secret doctrine, given only to those who had proved themselves ready to receive the inner truths of spiritual life from the Masters of the Wisdom. In the Egyptian mysteries, we learn of the exacting tests a candidate had to pass before he or she could be

---

the Word as the second person of the Trinity. In most instances White Eagle speaks of the Trinity as being 'Father, Mother, Son' and in the course of this book refers to the Mother as the second person. In view of White Eagle's usual phrase it might be less confusing to regard the Son as the third person. However, here the formula is of God as the first, the Word as the second, and the Wisdom of God as the third person.

'The Golden One' is in any case not to be regarded as male, but rather beyond the distinction of gender. Nevertheless, where White Eagle makes an association between the Golden One, the Christ, and therefore Jesus, we have allowed the simple male pronoun.

admitted into the holy of holies. Truth is ever the same, yesterday, today and for ever. The sacred mysteries of creation have always been preserved—yet at the same time withheld, until the aspirant has proved ready and worthy to witness the uncovering of these inner spiritual truths, which lie within the heart of religion, and are to be found in all that is most profound in philosophy and valuable in science.

The Jesus Christ of the Christian scriptures is really a twofold person, signifying the dual nature. That is, in one sense, the Master Jesus is a separate person who was a great master—or a messenger sent to earth by God to point the right way for humanity to live on earth. There have always been such messengers sent to us throughout the ages, and all of them have been born in similar circumstances and under the same astrological signs. Virgo is always in the ascendant at the time of their birth; the birth is always from a virgin (Virgo); and the sign of the lamb (Aries) always became the sign in space of the crucifixion. These sun-myths occur throughout the ages, as can be instanced from those of Osiris, Vishnu, and Quetzalcoatl (the Saviour of the American Indians). Cosmic mysteries such as these always gather round the latest divine teacher, and are apt to confuse the story of the glorious figure of the Christ, the 'true and only begotten Son of the Father'. For the Christ, who is the Golden One, is the Son–Daughter or the Sun of God; and is at-one with the divine parent, with the Creator. Yet He or She also is the creator of all things. The Golden One is the breath of life—indeed *is* Life. He–She manifests throughout nature, and in the highest form of life, in humanity. His–Her Light is in every heart. As it is written:

In the beginning was the Word, and the Word was with God, and the Word was God. The same was in the beginning with God. All things were made by him; and without him was not any thing made that was made. In him was life; and the life was the light of men. And the light shineth in darkness; and the darkness comprehended it not.... That was the true Light, which lighteth every man that cometh into the world. (Jn 1 : 1–5, 9)

As the glorious golden rays are clairvoyantly seen proceeding from the heart of the spiritual Sun (the sun behind the physical sun), so do they pierce the heart of everyone living in this world of matter. As the Christ said, *I am the light of the world. I am in the Father, and the Father in me* (Jn 8 : 12, 14 : 11).

The words spoken by the Christ are plain and clear truth, for those who have ears to hear. Christ was the hero of the ancient sun myths, for he was God's messenger to humanity; and through Jesus came the glorious and transcendent manifestation of the Golden One, the Son of God ... the Creator of Life, the Solar Logos. The Son of God descended into matter, and the sun is naturally his symbol, since the Sun is his body. He is often described as 'he that dwelleth in the sun'. This is the way he appears, as the human figure of a man, perfect and beautiful in every detail, enthroned in the heart of a blazing spiritual Sun. He is the Divine Intelligence, the bringer of life to the earth planet, for without the sun there would be no life. The story of the Transfiguration gives an indication of the glory and the power of this divine Sun life, which shone through and around Jesus. It was not the light of Jesus' own spirit which was seen by the frightened and awed disciples. It was the transcendent glory of the Solar Logos.

The mystical truth of the Trinity of God, the Father, Mother and Son, is one of the holy mysteries which is not fully understood until the veils are withdrawn from the eyes of the soul in future initiations. We can but glimpse and believe in the divine Omnipresence, the Omniscience and the Omnipotence, which manifest to the aspiring soul in varying degrees of spiritual beauty.

Humanity has to be convinced of the gentle human

qualities of this Spirit, for these qualities have been portrayed through the messengers who have come to earth from God through all the past ages, who have brought to humanity the true wisdom in all religions. In this teaching there is always the same inner truth, the foundation of which is encompassing love, goodwill, and the universality of all life—the at-one-ment with God, the eternal Spirit. For the Christ-spirit, which is both alpha and omega, is the one and only saviour of human kind. What would the world be like today if this Christ-spirit were the supreme ruler in every organized body formed to do good to humanity; in every group or church, great or small; in every institution and in all governments and political organizations throughout the world? What would happen were the vision of the perfection of the Golden One placed before every healing institution, and became the focal point in every hospital, university and science laboratory? Would not the world become a better place, and would not humanity then have its feet placed firmly upon the path leading to perfect life?

This may perhaps be regarded as an impossible ideal; nevertheless, this was the ideal that Jesus Christ gave to the world, and it is through the lack of this true vision that the people suffer and perish. How then can men and women come to the hilltop from which they can glimpse the glory of this panorama of a golden age, governed by the Golden One? Only by daily aspiration, and practice of the simple Christlike way of life. They must not wait for 'the other person' to put into practice the precepts of the Sermon on the Mount; they must set to work to do to others as they would like to be done to themselves.

Yes, it is the gentle human qualities which are the things seen and loved in Jesus the Christ, and in all the saints who have lived on earth to do His will. Jesus Christ said, *Not every one that saith unto me, Lord, Lord, shall enter into the kingdom of heaven; but he that doeth the will of my Father which is in heaven* (Mt 7 : 21). This same gentle and human as well as divine spirit is what we see revealed in the Golden One when our heart centre opens wider and yet wider in pure love for God and all Creation. The Golden One is not remote from any soul, but is warm, friendly, understanding, and comforting to everyone who, in childlike trust and faith, turns to Him–Her in the secret chamber of the heart. What is then discovered in the simple, human and loving heart is all truth; it is cosmic truth, for then the inner light points the way upwards to the heavens, to the Solar Logos, and to the Cosmos itself. For it is there, *there*, that the child of God sees with clear unfaltering vision the Divine Heart, the centre from which all life proceeds, pouring forth through all eternity the Light and the Life of the Son, 'The Golden One.'

With such thoughts as these deeply pondered in our minds we return to our meditations.

The Christ Presence

You can come into the very presence of the Golden One if you will do your seeking in childlike simplicity and humility. If you can do this you will absorb all wisdom, love and power. You will become at-one with all life. You will realize the cosmic consciousness. Even now you are not separate from life; you are in it; you are a part of every creature; you are the universe itself....

When you can enter into that cosmic life in full spiritual consciousness you will feel the strong support of the Golden One, and all fear, all weariness and all restlessness will leave you.

We want you to know and believe that there is such a Presence, that this glorious power is personified. You may be like a drop in the ocean, or a grain of sand on the shore, but your spirit is still a part of the supreme One.

You worship the Christ not knowing whom or what you worship. You clothe Christ in your own thoughts, your own ideas. That is the best you can do. You must know the love of Christ; you seek, in your meditations, to feel yourself resting in the heart of Christ. Then you will see your earthly life in its true perspective; and your work also; and your friends.

The perfect love of the Golden One is your staff through life. It will sustain you on your earthly journey as you climb the mountains of toil and difficulty, right up to the highest until you come at last into the golden Presence. To the person who loves God all works together for good.

Breathe in the divine life, absorb into your being the radiance of the great Sun, and go about your life and your work in physical matter, warm and radiant in the Golden One, the Sun, the lifegiver.

When the will to become Christlike grows strong in the heart, it causes an opening in the consciousness for the greater self to descend into the physical body.

You think that your physical body is you, but it is only an infinitesimal part of you.

If you would contact your true self, go into a place of quiet to commune with your Creator in your heart. Then you will rise in consciousness. That great Light to which you rise is, you will find, the divine self; you, yourself, your own divinity, the real you. By opening your consciousness to this divine self all your vibrations will be quickened and your body will become purified.

Never be afraid. The greatest enemy of human kind is fear. Be confident in the love and the wisdom of God; darkness will not touch you if you are radiating light. Light is love and purity and all the qualities of the Christ-spirit.

May the divine Will sleeping within you rise and direct your life.

Meditation

Now may the Holy Grail, your heart, be filled with Light divine.

Hold your heart open like a cup that it may be filled with the golden Liquid, the essence of life....

Rest in the Lord

Always the Master forgives and understands, but you cannot reach the Master until you have learnt to discipline the emotions. Unruly emotions are a barrier to reaching the plane of the Master. By your love and your persistence in the gentle, calm way, you too will do much to help your companions. But remember always that control of the emotions is of paramount importance if you wish to keep your holy contact with your Master; and when there is a fiery uprising within you, try to send it forth instead in warm, sweet, tender love. This is not easy; but if the path were easy the prize would not be so great. It is because the path is difficult, and because tests have to be faced and overcome, that the reward is so fine. The two go hand in hand.

The secret of strength lies in the quiet mind. When tempted to become worried, disturbed, anxious, fearful, turn your thoughts to the still places, saying, *The Lord is my shepherd; I shall not want; He restoreth my soul; He leadeth me beside still waters; He maketh me to lie down in green pastures...* (Ps 23).

Remember, the Lord your God is the shepherd; God will not forsake you.

You must learn to accept your path, walking not only with humility, but with knowledge that the Master's way is the right way, even though it leads up hill, as well as down dale. Have you not had proof? For your way has often been difficult and obscure, yet you will confess that the Lord is good, wise, loving.

Seek then for the quiet mind, for in the eternal peace of God your Father and your Mother shall be your strength.

If you can think of yourself as being all that you know you should be: constant, gentle, loving and kind to every man, woman and child, and to every circumstance in life; kind and tolerant in your attitude towards all conditions on earth; above all, if you can conceive yourself as being completely calm in all conditions and circumstances, quiet and yet strong—strong to aid your weaker brethren, strong to speak the right word, to take the right action, and so become a tower of strength and light; if you can see yourself facing injustice and unkindness with

imagination is powerful

a serene spirit, knowing that all things work out in time for good, and that justice is always eventually triumphant; if you have patience to await the process of the outworking of the will of God: if you can picture becoming like this, you will know something of mastership.

Meditation

Picture an Elder Brother, as he stands before you now: he is of gentle presence, with golden brown hair, deep violet-blue eyes; about his head is a soft golden radiance, and upon his breast hangs a jewel which sends forth a dazzling, even rainbow-like, light. His raiment is white, girdled with gold set with jewels; upon his feet are sandals of gold. With him are other disciples, gentle, and full of love. Try to respond to them as their love enfolds you.... Silently commune with them as they draw near.

All that is sought from you, God's child, is the devotion of your heart; all God wants is your heart for God, your heart for all that is good. For God is love, and the soul that loves God knows God and does what God wills; thereafter to that soul all things are possible. Have patience and keep on working for God.

The love of the Golden One enfolds you.

The arms of the Golden One reach towards you and gather you into the golden heart....

Resurrection

The infinite Christ-spirit is ever present in your heart, and is the goodness and the gentleness of your own nature. When Christ, through Jesus, said *I am the resurrection and the life* (Jn 11 : 25), He referred not to life after death, but to more abundant physical life. Within your heart is the Light and beauty of the gentle Christ-spirit; it is this which is the resurrection and the life. Let it rise in you and use you, and speak through your lips; <u>let the ways of Christ be your ways</u>, and the gentle touch of Christ be yours in your daily life.

This beautiful pure God–Sun–spirit comes to recreate and heal you, and to perfect all the rough places in your life. Only surrender to this saving grace, this glorious spiritual power, and you will be healed of all infirmities; you will be comforted, and a great peace will come to you.

You enjoy the sunshine, you bask in it, and say how lovely it is; but it is only a gleam in comparison with the spiritual Sun. We ask you to rise in imagination above the limitation and the darkness of the earth plane into this Light of the Sun. Live in it, breathe it into your being; it is power, it is life, and can recreate you on every plane. No inharmony can live in that Light. In moments of fear and doubt, instantly attune yourself to the one true Light of life and invite it to command the situation; then you will overcome all things.

This creative Power, this mighty Presence, this blazing Light can and will banish and consume all inharmony. All ill-health and trouble in the outer life are due to lack of attunement to this Christ Sun.

Meditation

In the Golden Lodge is enthroned the Son of God, the Christ.

Receive, in the stillness, holy communion with the Christ.

Partake of the substance of the Christ body.

Sip the wine of the Christ-spirit.

Be fed and strengthened by the divine food for both mind and spirit....

The Christ comes before you ... comes very close. The Light arises from within you, and blazes forth all over the earth....

'I AM the Light of the world. Receive me....'

The Golden One is blessing you, is with you.

Amen.

CHAPTER 8

Work with the Light

THE higher self of each human soul is symbolized by the six-pointed Star. At a distance of between ten and fifteen feet above you, see this shining Light, which is in reality your higher self. Paul called it the 'celestial' body. Perhaps you cannot believe that you possess such a vehicle? But it is so, and it is attached to your outer self by what is called the silver cord. Down this silver cord there come into your body light-atoms to preserve it in harmony, in health, in vital force. When there comes a closing of the door in your physical consciousness through your refusal to believe and have faith in the spiritual life, less and less of this vital force can enter. Then the silver cord, which is like a lifeline, grows finer and thinner until there is a shutting-off of vital force. When the spirit can no longer give life the body falls away into what is called death.

This end is not your Creator's plan for any of the sons and daughters of God. You are intended to inherit the divine life which your Father–Mother God wishes you to manifest on earth. The whole purpose of your mortal life in this body is that you may, perhaps after repeated incarnations, manifest the Christ within in your outer life. You are God's child; you come down here to do a piece of work. That work is to manifest this Christ Light through the flesh.

The Master Soul

We have told you that when we speak of Light we mean God. God is love. Light is love. Does this seem to be no more than an ideal? But love *is* an ideal. We want you to understand that through your mind and the emotions of every day you can utilize the substance which is called Light. Indeed, you are already utilizing it by taking it and moulding it in your bodies.

How can you become more conscious of your work with the Light? We stress again the truth that you are masons, you are builders, and your building material is soul-substance and Light. This Light can be released in you. All visible creation is Light in form. Every form of matter is fundamentally Light. All life is vibration and according to the quality or rate of vibration the Light takes differing forms. You must awaken to the truth that God is Light, and that you are Light; and that you have been given working tools with which to build your temple of Light. These working tools are your body, your emotions, your thoughts—

physical, astral, mental. You will have to learn to use these tools if you want to build your temple. Then, when in due course you have graduated, you will appear as a beautiful and perfect jewel, the master-soul.

In the early stages of spiritual development it is both helpful and wise to ponder on the miracle of the growth and unfolding of a flower. There is yet another miracle in the withdrawal of life from physical or material form. Both aspects need to be considered and meditated upon.

We would speak to you of something even more wondrous than the miracle of the flower. We would direct your thoughts to the miracle of the development of the spiritual nature: the spiritual unfoldment taking place in the soul. Would that we could find words with which to picture the glory of the form of a master-soul. We can give you perhaps an inkling of this wonder by describing that form as being like a jewel. Think of a jewel-box; then imagine that you open your casket, and see, lying upon a soft cushion within, a golden jewel flashing light like fire and dazzlingly beautiful. Light from the rays of this jewel goes forth in all directions, high and broad and deep. Conceive this in your mind's eye—a perfect, flashing jewel. Try to obtain from this some idea of the glory of a master-soul.

Keep this ideal ever before you, remembering that *you*, in spite of all limitations and failures, are created to become some day like that jewel. For as the bulb planted in the dark soil eventually raises its head to the sunlight as a flower, so every human soul contains within its being the potential qualities of becoming a master-soul, a perfect jewel.

Meditation

Try earnestly to feel within your heart the truth of what we tell you. In your meditation try to conceive this ideal of the flashing golden jewel. Within that jewel is to be seen the perfect human form.

This perfect form is the perfected son–daughter of God.

This is you! This is also your ideal.

The Graph of the Spiritual Life

You must learn to subdue, to purify, to order all your thoughts. You must learn to control desires and emotions, and create in your higher nature an ideal, by proceeding from the physical through the astral and the mental into the sphere of ideation. There your ideal becomes manifest, your mission accomplished. Afterwards you can descend again through the planes back to the earth. Spiritual development through meditation can be likened to a graph, rising and falling, rising and falling. You start from the bottom and climb to the heights; you leave the heights and descend to the bottom. All the while you are growing in spirit, because of your spiritual experience.

Do not give up hope; do not be timorous; know yourself as you are; recognize your failings and your weaknesses, but have courage enough to believe that every effort you put forth is something accomplished. It does not matter if you fail, because you cannot yourself judge. Failure in your eyes can often be achievement from the spiritual point of view.

Strive to become a good scholar and pupil. If you make mistakes, do not despair. The very fact that you are continually trying shows that you are already on the way. If not, you would have given up before. The fact that you can create an ideal and follow it shows that you are ready.

The soul that is carried to the heights is bound to descend again. At times you will feel full of spiritual ecstasy and ready for anything; at others you feel hopeless. Never, never mind. Hold on with a loving heart both to your ideal and to your Father–Mother God, the Parents who are ever watching over you, who ever understand Their child because They have given you birth. Keep on persevering. Regard this everyday life as your set of lessons. You are thereby bringing the light within into conscious operation, so that in time the very cells of your body become impregnated with it. This is what is happening in the outer world as well. Spirit (or God) is continually renewing, purifying and thereby raising the world-vibrations. Physical matter is the densest substance of all, a raw material which waits to be moulded by the master-builders.

Meditation

Let us for meditation take the picture of the arisen Christ. Visualize the golden disc of the Sun, and the perfect form of the Christ, with outstretched arms within the heart of this golden radiance. ...

As the arms are raised to give blessing, the words are spoken, *I, if I be lifted up ... will draw all ... to me....* (Jn 1 2 : 32).

The Word of God

To work consistently with the Light, withdraw your consciousness, your thoughts and emotions from the outer world; turn steadfastly to the inner world, the home of spirit; and in this world that is so still—and yet the centre and source of all outward form and life—you will strike the one tremendous Note which we will call the Word of God.

In the beginning was that Word; and the Word was with God. *Light*! That Word was God.

First turn within. In the silence the Word is heard, and that Word is the First Cause. This is what the aspirants seek. They withdraw from the world. They climb the snow-clad peaks to meditate and to hear the Word. The nearest sound to that Word that human beings can comprehend is the hum of life, which is interpreted as 'Aum'. Feel that vibration stirring within you. Feel that the seed-atom of God is within your heart. Then, as you say that Word physically, mentally, emotionally you are releasing the life and the light within.

The Elder Brethren are in our midst, here and

now. May your inner eyes behold them. Remember, they have bodies of pure light vibrating at a very high rate. That is why they are beyond the range of physical sight, but are close to you in spirit. They promise you their help as you aspire, and as you gain confidence in them so you will receive more help. Never put them from your mind. They are not remote. They are wholly understanding of you and your needs. They are only too happy to help with your labours in the world. Remember also the God within, which, if you call upon it and at the same time endeavour to let your lower mind stand on one side, will take possession and work through you. Thus you will be building, creating the temple of your soul. The Brethren give to you all their love, their blessing, in this great and selfless task.

Within, my children—deep, deep within—beneath all ungoverned thought and emotion, you will find the living Breath of spiritual life; the source of all healing and the source of eternal life.

So may the glory of the heavens irradiate and bless you.

Meditation

And now from our Elder Brethren we rise to the highest, to our Lord and Master Christ and to the Father–Mother God, the holy and blessed Trinity, the Source of our being.... We worship, we worship, we glorify Thee, and Thy blessing is upon Thy children. We thank Thee for the glory of the spiritual life....

For the happiness and the beauty which all Thy gifts bring to Thy children in all the worlds in which they are placed....

Thy peace broods over us....

Amen. Amen. Amen.

Faith

Cherish a constant and ever-present faith in God's love and mercy. Fight against all negative thought. An unseen army of darkness—we call them brethren of the shadow—swarms among humanity; and these denizens of the shadow seek to put weakening and fearful thoughts into your minds. They come to test you, and thereby to help strengthen your inner light. As such negative thoughts crowd in day by day, cast them out. Strive after God-thought, positive thought, loving thought. Be undeterred by the denizens of the shadow, who speak sometimes to you through the lips of other men and women. Hold fast to the God-life; create for yourself a harvest of Light; not with hope of self-gain, but knowing that as you work within yourself towards the Light and beauty of God, you are working for all humanity.

Overcome fear. Fear—on every plane—is the greatest enemy, and must be overcome. Have no fear; the God within you and enfolding you is all power, and the love you project from your heart, sincere, pure and gentle, protects you, for it is the shield and armour of the Knight of the Grail. Meditate upon this.

Meditation

There appears a vision of the Master Jesus walking on the surface of the water. We see in our meditation the sea of Galilee. We are in a boat, rowing towards him, and so great is our love for the Master that we cry out. He sees us, and bids us step out of the boat and walk towards him on the water. Forgetting ourselves and our heaviness, we step out of the boat and walk on the surface of the water even as he does. No thought of fear or failure comes to us until we are so close to him that he can touch us; then realization of our position enters our minds and fear causes us to start sinking, but he stretches forth his hand, and by his touch, confidence is restored in us, because we have faith, an inner certainty, that he will strengthen our confidence and uphold us. His spirit renews the faith within ourselves.

Another picture comes. We are on the top of a high cliff, and we overbalance, falling over the edge. We are not afraid because we know that not being in a physical body, we cannot be hurt. With this thought we find ourselves landing gently and unharmed upon the soft mossy ground. This is a lesson in faith.

A third and last symbol is given in our meditation. We find ourselves ascending a road leading to a golden temple, the entrance to which is guarded on either side by ferocious wild beasts. Dare we pass them to enter this hall of initiation?

We are alone and must rely upon our own courage and faith in the master or guardian of that magnificent temple.

We believe there is an unseen power guiding and guarding us. We see the light shining out through the door of the temple. We go forward, passing the two ferocious beasts courageously, and to our amazement they only come up to us to lick our outstretched hands. We have passed the test of *faith*.

Let there be Light!

Spring is the appointed time for the great Mother to manifest her love, her beauty and her wisdom. Others are associated with the great Mother; these are the devas, the great angels and the planetary beings. There are also sun-spirits, sylphs, and spirits of the air, which come with the spirits of the fire. The sun-spirits come with great joyous songs which cleanse and revivify the life stored within the earth. All are under the rule of the sun gods who have brooded over human kind since the beginning of life. This mighty company watches over the destinies of human beings and of nations. They have always been concerned with the spiritual growth and evolution of humanity, and on them rests the ordering of the natural forces of the earth.

On occasions it has been found necessary to purify the surface of the earth. This is when the dark forces become so strong and violent that the equilibrium of the planet is disturbed, a state which comes about when people become dominated by selfish aims and cruel passions, or when they seek to gain power over others through exercise of occult forces.

Because of this the Great Ones continually watch over humanity, waiting for any entrance into the human consciousness, so that they can guide men and women to return to the one true path of spiritual achievement, the path of the Sun ... the Light and life which brings beauty, unity and order in the natural and animal kingdoms, and the gentle Christ life in the human kingdom. The world today needs your help, and that of every aspiring man and woman. Much depends upon each individual effort to project the spiritual sunlight, the Light of Christ, into the earthly life, for as yet there are few who can project this Light with knowledge, certainty and power.

Long ago the mystic words went forth, *Let there be Light!* There is a vibration from the heart of God which radiates Light; when you have realized your union with that Light within your innermost being, you will understand the power of those words. Then you too will send forth a vibration into the denser ether interpenetrating the physical plane.

Such sending forth from your broadcasting house is more potent than any action.

Learn to project Light and love continually, not from your lips but from the powerhouse within your innermost being.

Meditation

Now resign yourselves in tranquillity to the magic presence of God.

From within your heart, feel the babe, the Christ-child stirring; feel love welling forth for those about you, for all men and women, for nature and for animals....

Now let your heart centre expand. This is growth of the Christ babe. In your meditation you will become more and more aware of this expansion and will know that a radiance is going from you, a blessed compassion, a love and a Light which heals. And as you send forth, so also will you draw in additional Light from your celestial body, so that that which you give, you will also receive. In the measure that you give, so shall you receive.

Begin from the heart of life; have full confidence in the great and sacred powers of love, which are closely waiting for your co-operation, your union with them.

By an effort of the divine will within, direct the spiritual Light and power out into the world, to lighten the darkness of the world...

To ease the pain of all who suffer....

To inspire thoughts of goodwill in human hearts....

To bring peace and brotherhood amongst the nations.

May the divine magic work in and through your hearts and lives, for the blessing of human kind, and the glory of your Father–Mother God in heaven.

Conservation

We would impress upon you the need for the conservation of energy. We think, at the autumn season, of the Divine Mother, that Second Principle of life, the Mother Principle of the deity, whose form is all-embracing. The Divine Mother enfolds and draws into Herself, conserving in the womb of life. The Father Principle is action and will and the giving forth of life, but the Mother enfolds and conserves. At this time of the year this Mother Principle is emphasized, for we see in nature the drawing in, the conserving of the life-forces before the next outbreathing, the birth of life in the spring.

You must learn to conserve energy and to control the emotional and mental expenditure and wastage that continually takes place in everyday life. A Master has learned the supreme lesson of the conservation of energy; he or she will never waste it, the vital force, the God-life. A Master trains himself, herself, to remain calm and tranquil in spite of the storms of life.

A Master knows that the greatest power and capacity to achieve comes from making contact calmly and steadily with the eternal Source of life and strength. Be still. Do not be buffeted about by the demands of the world. Be the master of your own life and conditions. Accept with calm fortitude the karma you have created. Rise above it. See the joy coming to you from your experiences. There is beyond the present condition a perfect state for you. If you are devoid of love, yet love is there, waiting, and it will some day fill your life, perhaps sooner than you think. The Master who watches you through your appointed guide has infinite love for you; and although the blows may seem hard at times, yet, in the degree you can withstand them, knowing there is a wise purpose behind every happening, you will find the place of strength, of the silence, of the inner power which is life eternal. Concentrate on the Light and the life of God, and the walls of your prison will melt. Hold fast to the certainty that God is love and that all is working towards a beautiful culmination. Accept all, and conserve within you this unseen life, this unseen energy, knowing divine peace, knowing divine love. This is the creative power. It is this power which will create for you the happy conditions for which you long. Life is unfoldment. Life is living in God, is surrendering to God's love. Do your part and do not worry about what the other person does, for it is not your concern, except to give them a helping hand if they ask for it.

This is the lesson to be learned from nature at this season, the withdrawing into the silence of the womb of life, there conserving the seed, protecting it in readiness for the putting forth of fresh life, fresh effort.

Meditation

We would raise your consciousness from the outer world to the spirit worlds. To open your meditation we would ask you to concentrate on the eastern sky lit by the dawn, on the rising sun and the stillness of vast mountains. Then we would take you into the golden temple which is not seen by mortal eyes but only by the celestial vision....

Quietly and in prayer come with us into this golden temple and enter the presence of the Golden One, who is all-peace and utter stillness. Absorb from the Golden One this peace of eternity and infinity....

Then the burdens of the flesh slip away, for you enter into a state of life which has no burdens. You are touching a level of consciousness that is your true and eternal life. At this level you experience nothing but joy and peace, beauty and love.

The Mystic Rose

The rose is a fragrant blossom, and comes to perfection at the time of the summer solstice. It is often used as a symbol of love. In the ancient, the timeless Brotherhood, the rose is held as a sacred symbol of attainment, of passing the highest degree possible while you are in the flesh. The rose is the symbol of the perfected soul; and the perfected soul is very faintly recognized by humanity as the Son of God, the Christ-spirit, the highest attainment possible by a soul on this earth.

In this ageless Brotherhood, which was yesterday, is today and will be for evermore, there is a sign which all the Brethren understand. The Brethren say, 'May the rose bloom upon your cross'. Those who understand the symbolism know that they mean, 'May you as my brother–sister in spirit so live your life, that instead of your being stretched upon the cross of pain and suffering, the rose shall bloom at your heart, the rose shall cover your cross'. In other words, you, the soul, shall be triumphant over all the limitations of life on earth. If you visualize the human figure standing with arms outstretched, you will see that it forms the cross. In the centre of the breast is the heart. That heart is radiant in glory; it is the rose blooming in the centre of the cross!

Meditation

We leave the earth and rise in spirit, seeking a garden of roses.

We observe the perfect form, colour and perfume of the innumerable blooms, and select the most perfect, the one that appeals to us most. We meditate upon its colour and form and inhale its fragrance. It seems like the essence of Christ's spirit, and we see in its heart the face of the Lord Christ as we personally conceive it.

This develops into the form of the perfect being, with head upraised and arms stretched out in the act of blessing.

He raises us up from dark earthiness by His love.

Upon the centre of His breast flowers the rose....

We see it in the place of His heart....

We hear the words, 'The sorrows of your life shall bloom like roses, and you shall see them in the garden of your spirit home'.

Hymn

O God, where beauty is, Thou art,
Within the chalice of the Rose;
Within the temple of my heart
Thy kingdom grows.

Thy will hath caused the seed to be,
Thy breath hath summoned at its hour
The living beauty from the tree,
This lovely flower.

O Rose of God, awake and live
A flame of beauty in my sight;
Shine from this heart that I may give
Thy perfect light.

T.D.

PART III

CHAPTER 9

The Rose Star

IN THE early part of 1946 instructions were received that a group of people should be joined under the symbol of the rose and star and, working under certain spiritual conditions which would raise the group consciousness, receive particular guidance on the matter of meditation and spiritual unfoldment. The first meeting was on Easter Day, April 21st, 1946.

It is in the belief that the Master's words of wisdom and instruction on the path towards spiritual attainment should be shared by those who are willing to receive and accept them, and that his aura still pervades the written word to bless the reader, that the following extracts are given.

I

Men and women seek individualism because they seek self-consciousness, but later they learn that the way of God-consciousness is through the group. You think you are individuals. You think of yourselves as individuals, as monads, because you are learning expression on the outer plane, from the point of the triangle; but, my dear ones, you have yet to learn that you are part of a group. There are many members in that group, countless numbers. You, the individual, we liken to the proton, and around you circulate the electrons.

You must open your consciousness to this divine cosmic reality. You are nothing. Of yourselves you can do nothing. You cannot live alone. You have many selves, many personalities. You belong to your group, and your group belongs to many other groups, which form a community: and that community belongs to many other communities which form a sphere, and so on and on.

Every man or woman who thinks that he or

she is a sole individual and lives with this thought of self-life is living in darkness. Humanity is learning by the hard way this truth of group life, of brotherhood, of co-operation, and expansion of the little consciousness into the God-consciousness. The only way you can realize this is through pure love.

Look up into the heavens and see this truth demonstrated in the myriad stars....

I am nothing....

I am all when I recognize all.

II

In the beginning was the Word, and the Word was with God, and the Word was God.... (Jn 1 : 1)

And God said, Let there be Light: and there was Light.... (Gen 1 : 3)

... and from the Light everything was made. I AM that Light. ... Light is the substance of life, of everything there is. And the Light is with all people.

The secret of the control of matter in all forms and on all planes lies in the pure love of the son—daughter of God in you. It is called by some the Presence of God. The saints and early brother-hoods spoke of the Presence of God within them and in their lives; others called this Presence the I AM within. The Lord Jesus Christ spoke of this Light, this life. He said: *Before Abraham was, I AM* (Jn 8 : 58). I AM the beginning and the end; I AM the circle; I AM alpha and omega. ... I AM....

This is the truth that every brother, every sister finds: the Presence, God, the Son, the Christ, the Life, the Light.

May your lives be both guided and inspired by this Divine Presence. May you worship no other God but the Light within. ... And then, my brothers, my sisters, after many days, you may bring forth the beau-tiful Light, the Shekinah.

III

You cannot attain to full stature through mind alone. Knowledge will come when the mind in the heart is trained to think. Only in brotherhood can this mind in the heart learn to function. We have worked in the past with this power, the sacred White Light which is generated from the heart. First, before the centre of *kundalini* is touched, it must be developed in the heart, where lies the key to the mysteries—the key which unlocks the gate of initiation into the divine mysteries. The brotherhood must be realized and felt and spontaneously lived.

The revealer of the secrets of all the kingdoms of nature is within yourself; and the way to unlock the door of the mysteries is by meditation, simplicity, purity, humility and love.

Be unperturbed by what looks like failure. All things can happen through faith in the Lord Christ. Miracles are the natural outworking of a spiritual law not understood by the people of earth, the people of clay. Be strong in spirit and thus you will overcome the being of earth who is your enemy. The one who rules the kingdom of the lower mind, this is your greatest enemy; be resolute in your determination to overcome this being of clay.

IV

Beauty of life, devotion to God, courage in adversity, calm joyousness in prosperity, perfect balance in the life and unswerving loyalty to the Brotherhood and the cause for which we all work, these we ask of you. We do not make fair promises to you. We only convey to you what we know, that by loving Christ, by following the example of Jesus and others of our Brotherhood who have set that example on earth, you, with others, will attain supremacy over the physical life and know the sweetness of the heavenly life and of service to one another and to all humanity.

Never forget that you were created to become a king or queen, and ruler of your own realm, God's realm. You are a monarch; you have this noble destiny. Therefore you must develop the will to be as God, the will to be as God's son–daughter … the will … I will … I WILL BE … I AM….

Practise this in your life: Supreme rulership of your own kingdom.

But practise it with the gentleness and sweetness and humility of Christ.

V

Beloved brethren, we bring you sweet love. Take courage, for behind you is a greater power than you realise.

Strive to overcome the weakness of the flesh. Be patient, be trusting.

Give yourselves to the spirit in patience and humility, whatever your calling. Be constant in your service to the brotherhood of life.

We know human weakness; we understand your difficulties, but we do not excuse them. We understand, but we ask you to strive daily towards perfection.

Keep the Light burning. There is nothing more important on earth than to keep the Sun Light and the Christ Light burning. Only this will give you the power that you need to do those little acts of service that the Master asks of you.

As you work with courage and patience in your particular corner of the earth, so will you be rewarded by the ever-increasing consciousness in yourselves of the companionship and the very real help in your material lives, given to you by your invisible helpers.

VI

There is no death, only death of that which is igno-rant; but to those who rise from the grave of ignorance and darkness and earthliness there is no death. The very cells of the physical body are con-tinually being reborn, recreated, for the process of life is creation, and a continual perfecting. This is the secret of the philosopher's stone, the secret of making pure gold. Not only the knowledge which comes to the earthly mind, but the love in the heart of the brother or sister, the life of the Sun in the heart-temple, is the power which creates and changes the form and substance of things visible and invisible.

With hands upraised, we bless you....

Your hands are symbols of blessing. Remember that you can bless human kind with your hands. They are sacred. See to it that your actions harmonise so that they use your hands in holy service to your brother or sister. Remember that though your hands may have to labour with menial tasks, through them may flow the blessing of God. Your hands may heal the sick. From your hands the holy Light pours forth. May every touch of yours be a blessing upon your companions....

VII

Do not allow the petty small things, which weary and disturb those who do not know what *you* know, to disturb the stillness of the lake of your consciousness. If you do, you fail to be servants of the Master.

You must know at all times that God, the Eternal Light, is Master of your destiny. Yours is not to question but to accept the way as it opens before you, having complete confidence in the love and the wisdom of those who are your companions, the companions of your spirit.

Your task is simple but not easy. Be one-pointed; be true to your higher self. *I, if I be lifted up, will raise all men unto me....* (Jn 1 2 : 3 2). An age-old truth.

Fix your heart and mind upon the symbol of our brotherhood, the Rose Star. Absorb it: be one with it.

No longer I, but Thou.... Thou art That....

In this consciousness dwell all the Great Ones of the past, the present and the future; a goodly company.

We are the circle of Light. The arms of the cross form from the north to the south, from the east to the west, and in the centre is the Rose....

So may the roses bloom upon the cross of mortal life for all true brethren of the Rose Star.

Brethren, let us send forth the Star of the Rose to those who are at war with one another, whether as people, whether as nations; let us bring forth Light out of the darkness....

So mote it be.

Be calm, be tranquil, dear children, and you will be happy. You must find the secret of happiness before you can impart it to others.

Sorrow is akin to happiness. Out of your sorrow and grief will be born joy and happiness. Happiness will surely follow sorrow as day follows night.

The Elder Ones bless you and tenderly love you. Think of their love for you and it will help you upwards. They know your need: the supply is limitless.

VIII

To suffer, yet not to suffer—the mystery of the Holy Grail.... Seek the Holy Grail; then be interpreters of the Word; give bread and wine to the people of earth.

Spare not yourselves; purify yourselves that you may taste and see for yourselves the glory of the heavens ... only thus can you feed the lambs, the children, coming up from darkness to the Light.

No one suffers who is with God. Jesus, when he hung upon the cross, did not suffer. He detached himself from the earth plane. Only the lower nature suffers. The body need feel no pain.

Behold the saints! Only through earthly imagination do they appear to suffer. They live to glorify the Father–Mother; and as they are in God and the God in them, they know not pain but only the joy and ecstasy of the life of the Father–Mother.

This is the way for all disciples of the Light ... detachment from the earth. And yet being alive in earth, glorify the earth, glorify the body!

IX

Whatever you are called upon to do, your method will always be the same; your vision set upon the Star, your heart fragrant with the Rose.

Go into the world with a secret mission; not to be pious, but to be a brother–sister to every soul whom you encounter; to live with others and share their joys and their experiences, but always by the gentle divine essence of love from your heart to uplift, to illumine and to help your companions on the path leading to freedom and happiness.

Meditation can be practised even in the kitchen amongst the pots and pans, as well as in the field and garden. Meditation can be practised in everyday life, but it can also be practised in the chapel, in the prepared chamber....

When you withdraw from the earth plane and you come up into the mountain heights with our Lord and Master, you forget the existence of the clay. Only thus will you be able to see Him when He comes into your midst.

Now He comes ... radiant with love, compassion,

tenderness, and beauty....

The outpouring of Light from His Being, from His hands, His heart, His head, is like the rays of the sun, warm and life-giving, beautifying.

Through you the same Light manifests in a lesser degree. This is in your life; it is for you to demonstrate the power of this life on earth, so that, being raised to heaven, you may raise all with you....

So mote it be!

X

This is the resurrection morn, the spiritual resurrection. He is living and is here now. He is in you. Remember this daily and say in your heart, *I AM the resurrection and the life.*

This is the secret wisdom, but no word of ours can teach you the mighty power which is yours. You must discover it, each of you for yourself.

As you gaze upon the blazing Star of gold remember that, according to your practice of the spiritual life, so will the blazing Star become *you*, and you will become the blazing Star, when you have arisen from the grave of materiality. *I AM the resurrection and the life!* That blazing star is you.

As the sap rises in the tree at this time, so must the sap, the eternal Light, continually rise in you, in your physical as well as your spiritual bodies.

There is no death! There should be no death in the physical, but humanity has to learn the secret of eternal resurrection, even as the sap rises in the tree each year.

The elder companions, the saints, are with you. We are in the Golden Lodge. Hail! hail! hail! to the Sun!

See Him! hear Him! His heart is the Cup, the Holy Grail, filled with His spirit, His love.

'Take from Me.' He takes the Bread from His body ... My body. Blessed be the body of the Sun! O, Mighty One, bless this body, the bread for the children of Thy Spirit.

And He breaks the bread into many pieces and He

gives it to you to eat, the cosmic body of the Holy One.

From the sacred place of His heart He draws forth the Cup. ...

'Drink, drink; it is my blood, the wine of life; drink in remembrance of Me, the Sun, the Life of the world ... for as I was dead yet I live eternally, and what I do ye can do also....'

Amen.

Let all the fret of life depart from you, my children. You must learn this as all the saints of old have done. You must learn this secret, for we would have you live long on the earth. It is not the will of God that you should escape life on the physical plane. It is the will of God that you retain your physical body for as long as your spirit needs it. The secret of longevity lies in the spirit, for spirit fills all matter.

In everything there is spirit. The God-intelligence grows to the highest degree in the Son, the Christ. This must grow in you. Your spirit must fill every cell of your body.

You do not live by bread alone, but by air, by water, by spirit. Practise this secret way of life.

You are the Son–Daughter of God and all around you are the elements of which you are created, and you draw upon these elements for your physical needs. Remember this, and live well and long and nobly and gloriously.

Study the laws of nature. Live by nature's laws. Live by the fruits of the earth and the herbs of the earth for the cure of all ills of the body. Keep your heart fixed upon the eternal spirit, the blazing Star, the brightness of which humanity has not yet seen. Breathe it in, absorb it....

XI

Build me a Temple of Light. I am within the Body of Light. It is my universe. I am within my universe and it is life; it is Light; it is good; and all creatures of my universe are good. They are born from my heart. My heart is the womb of life; my heart is the Rose.

I am the Divine Mother. Come unto me, all my children of the Light. I will raise you up into the Temple of the eternal Son, my Son....

In the heart of the Temple the altar is built. The altar is the living Rose. The petals are the blooms of eternal life and all creatures are embraced within the bloom.

The flames of the eternal fires become manifest through increasing consciousness of this life, the life of the Rose in the heart of the perfected Son.

The symbol of the Star is given to you to convey to your finite minds the idea of the perfect balance between light and darkness, for this perfect balance is all light. In the perfect balance there is no darkness at all.

I AM the centre from which all things proceed. Find Me and you shall become free.

XII

He that is Love is with us ... all love....

We are in the heart of the Rose. The Rose rests

upon the Six-pointed Star....

We think, speak and act from the heart of the Rose. It rests upon the table of earth.

All gather round the table upon which is spread the white cloth in readiness for the feast....

And He comes: the Beloved comes ... and offers you the bread. Take; eat....

Look up! The golden liquid which flows from His heart is caught in the chalice of the heart, and you drink and live eternally. In this way you are changed and live evermore in the Light and the life of the Sun ... changed from earth into Light.

The physical body dissolves. The body of Light is created, each one according to the pattern of the Father–Mother–Son.

Be not weary of seeking eternal life. Behold, we show you the Way which is triumphant over death. We show you the Way to pass from the third to the fourth dimension. Follow, follow the Way.

THE WHITE EAGLE PUBLISHING TRUST is part of the wider work of the White Eagle Lodge, a meeting place or fraternity in which people may find a place for growth and understanding, and a place in which the teachings of White Eagle find practical expression. Here men and women may come to learn the reason for their life on earth and how to serve and live in harmony with the whole brotherhood of life, visible and invisible, in health and happiness.

Readers wishing to know more of the work of the White Eagle Lodge may write to the General Secretary, The White Eagle Lodge, New Lands, Brewells Lane, Liss, Hampshire, England GU33 7HY (tel. 01730 893300) or can call at The White Eagle Lodge, 9 St Mary Abbots Place, Kensington, London W8 6LS (tel. 020-7603 7914). In the Americas please write to Church of the White Eagle Lodge, P. O. Box 930, Montgomery, Texas 77356 (tel. 409-597 5757), and in Australasia to The White Eagle Lodge (Australasia), Willomee, P. O. Box 225, Maleny, Queensland 4552 (tel. 0754 944397). A variety of activities is held at all these addresses. For information you can visit our websites at the addresses http://www.whiteagle.org and http://www.saintjohns.org, and you can e-mail us on enquiries@whiteagle.org (UK) or sjrc@saintjohns.org (USA). All the White Eagle books are available by mail order from the above postal and internet addresses but try your local bookstore first.